WITHIN SACRED CIRCLES

WITHIN SACRED CIRCLES

MEDITATIONS AND MANDALA QUILTS

SUSAN TOWNER-LARSEN

The Pilgrim Press Cleveland, Ohio

The Pilgrim Press, 700 Prospect Avenue, Cleveland, Ohio 44115-1100
pilgrimpress.com
© 2004 Susan Towner-Larsen

Biblical quotations, unless otherwise noted, are from the New Revised Standard Version of the Bible, © 1989 by the Division of Christian Education of the National Council of Churches of Christ in the U.S.A., and are used by permission. Adaptations have been made for inclusivity.

Printed in China

09   08   07   06   05   04   5   4   3   2   1

Library of Congress Cataloging-in-Publication Data

Towner-Larsen, Susan, 1950–
     Within sacred circles : meditations and mandala quilts / Susan Towner-Larsen.
        p. cm.
     Includes bibliographical references (p.   ) and index.
     ISBN 0-8298-1533-3 (alk. paper)
     1. Mandala.   2. Meditation.   3. Mandala quilts.   I. Title.

BL2015.M3T69 2004
247—dc22
                                                            2003066039

Dedication

To my great-grandmother, Louise Worthington, who shared her birthday

with me and taught me every kind of "handiwork" she knew.

She was my inspiration and an endless source of love.

•

To my grandmothers, Mildred Austin and Lily Towner.

Thank you, Mimi, for always being the loving presence I need.

Thank you, Mom-Mom, for warm memories of your gentle spirit.

•

To my mom, Catherine Towner, still my best friend

and cherished quilting companion.

•

To my sister, Pat Hazen, not a quilter,

but I love you anyway!

•

Especially to my daughters, Kara and Krista.

Words will always fail to capture the immensity of my love for each of you.

•

And to Bob, thanks for loving me in spite of the quilting clutter!

•

CONTENTS

ACKNOWLEDGMENTS

Quilted mandalas are new on the scene of the art world. This book would not have been possible without the graciousness and expertise of the countless quilt artists who shared their innovative, beautiful quilts. My only regret is that all of them could not be included in these pages. My deepest thanks to each of you. Your brilliant artistry was my constant inspiration.

Thanks, too, to the Holy One who brings the numinous to life. May your Spirit shine forth from each center point and word.

INTRODUCTION

Mandalas began to work their magic on me many years ago. With flowery centers and intricate designs, the endless circles I drew as a child were more mandala-like than I knew. My doodling took on added meaning after a college psychology class. I was captivated by the Jungian assertions that mandalas could be used for healing and self-discovery. With renewed inspiration, my journals began to fill with mandalas, sometimes in vibrant colors, sometimes simple sketches. While in my thirties, mandalas faded into the background as I explored other areas of creativity: child-rearing, cross-stitch samplers, and traditional quilting. Not to be suppressed for long, however, mandalas reappeared in my life when I began meeting with a spiritual director.

As a Roman Catholic sister, my director quickly "blew away" all of my antiquated stereotypes of members of religious orders, beginning with being a feminist and artist in her own right (although she probably would not have used those labels).

And so it was that, while on a four-day silent retreat, my spiritual director reintroduced me to mandalas, inviting their creation at every turn and supplying art materials each day. On the first day of the retreat, laden with a large tablet, water color supplies, and instructions from Sister Mary to "Go and create a mandala!" I detoured briefly through the bookstore of the Grailville retreat center. As I maneuvered through the door, I was shocked to glance up and find, right in the center of the top bookshelf, displayed all by itself, a book entitled *Magic Quilted Mandalas!* Setting aside all that I was carrying, I stood right there and read page after page. Not only did I buy the book, but as soon as I returned home, I placed a phone call to the author, Sheila Finklestein—a resident of my own state!

Gracious woman that she is, Sheila waited through all of my explanations of serendipity and managed to discern my enthusiasm for her art and my gratitude for her ability to connect two wonderful worlds: mandalas and quilts. My good friend Barb Davis and I had just finished writing our book *With Sacred Threads: Quilting and the Spiritual Life* and had planned a fall retreat based on the connections between quilting and the spiritual life. We immediately invited Sheila, wonderful guru of wedge-filled mandalas, to join us as one of the quilting teachers. The other retreat teacher, Vikki Pignatelli, was in the midst of writing a book of her own, detailing her process for designing and adding curves to quilts (think "circles" and "swirls" and "spirals"—previously scarce in the quilting world and so important to my own dreams of mandala quilts). Spirit-filled and sparked with creative energy, that first Sacred Threads Retreat exceeded all dreams and expectations, connecting quilts, mandalas, and spirituality in previously unnamed, unexplored ways. The yearly retreat continues even today, as does my fascination with mandalas and circular designs, each in their own way giving birth to this book.

From around the world and across all times, circular symbols have been integral to centering one's spirit and to expressing wholeness and unity. The word "mandala" comes originally from the Sanskrit language and means "center" or "to have possession of one's essence."[1] Mandalas have been used for healing and self discovery (Carl Jung), for connecting to God (Hildegard of Bingen), for spiritual rituals (Navajo sand paintings), and for embodying the Holy (Tibetan Buddhist sand mandalas).

It is my hope that this book will connect the traditions, uses, and symbolism of mandalas with the spirituality of quilters and the stories of their mandalas. Each chapter is based on a theme common to mandalas and to the spiritual life. Along with each reflection on the theme is a picture of a quilted mandala, the story of the quilt as told by its creator ("Sacred Story"), plus some prayers, holy text, and suggestions for meditation or for making your own mandala ("Sacred Meditation").

Even if your first inclination is to say "I can't draw," I encourage you to gather around you some colorful pencils, watercolor paints, or pastels. Make room for the Spirit to move you with the delight of color! Be prepared for bursts of unexpected creativity and the inspiration to express some deeply held feelings. No one but you (and the Holy One) will be watching. Be gentle with yourself and avoid any self-judgment about your art work. Just be and create.

If you are a seamstress or quilter, consider making fabric mandalas. The bibliography contains several excellent books on different methods for doing so. One simple process would be to gather a variety of fabric textures and colors. Cut twelve-inch by twelve-inch squares of each and back them with a fusible interfacing. From these prepared squares, you will be able to cut shapes for your mandalas as inspiration leads you. Draw a circle on a square of muslin before you begin the "Mandala Making" meditation. Using this circle as the base, as you are inspired, cut and add fabric. Later, after you have your images and the fabric shapes settled in place, fuse them with the iron, then appliqué, if desired, by your favorite method.

Each chapter concludes with "Sacred Meditation," offered as a time of contemplation. If you don't already have one, consider creating a sacred space for meditating—perhaps including your favorite chair, a small table with a candle, and any icons or natural items that connect you to the Holy (stones, leaves, incense, a piece of art, or a favorite book, for example). Of course, keep those art and/or fabric supplies nearby, too.

Art opens our souls to the Sacred. May the artistry of the quilted mandalas offered in these pages lead you to ever deepening connections to the Holy One and to celebration of the many sacred circles within which your life rests.

• Meditation •

andalas speak to my soul. I need only to look at one to feel my spirit begin to breathe, to come to a sense of calmness, a sense of being "home." Captivating in their beauty and their timeless symbolism, mandalas offer me a "sacred energy" for meditating and for finding my way back to my center, back to the Holy. Joan Borysenko, medical doctor and modern mystic, characterizes the essence of mandalas in these words:

> Mandalas are archetypes, or cosmic blueprints, for the Higher Self. They have been used for thousands of years, in both Eastern and Western traditions, as means for awakening. . . . In Tibetan Buddhist tradition, mandalas are considered to be the vibrational fields of deities. In meditating upon them, one aligns with that sacred energy.[1]

Sitting down at my quilt frame also aids my awakening and my alignment with all that is sacred. Putting needle and thread to cloth connects me, in some mystical,

I

unexplainable way, to my foremothers, women of faith and wisdom on whom I call for grounding and support, for recentering my very being. Inherent in the quilting process are other aspects of meditation as well: quiet opportunity for prayer; the discipline of making time for myself and God; openness to communities of women—past, present, and future; the expressing of my God-given creativity; an avenue for telling my story and expressing my "voice"; and time for healing, joy, and forgiveness to work into my soul.

Quilted mandalas combine the spiritual energy and meditative practices of these two artistic, timeless worlds: the world of mandalas and the world of quilts. The combination is powerful indeed!

In our everyday world, there exist many different forms of meditation, most intended to still the mind and center one in the presence of God, or a sense of the Holy.

Letting go of random thoughts and awakening to the Sacred is not necessarily easy or natural for us. Intentionality, practice, and guidance are often required. Books, mentors, icons, mandalas, spiritual directors/teachers/writers, retreats, gurus, faith traditions and communities—all are available for those who seek ways to meditate, awaken, and deepen their connections to all that is sacred.

For anyone exploring meditation for the first time, however, my suggestion is this: Be gentle with yourself. Created in the image of God, you already have within you wisdom and light, waiting to be gently uncovered or powerfully birthed. The key, Dr. Fontana points out, is focus. "Only with constant practice does the mind begin to learn how to focus. . . . One of the first steps toward focusing attention is simply to sit quietly and still the body, and then to become aware of distracting thoughts."[2] Distracting thoughts will come, most certainly. Do not be discouraged. "Notice" them, and then let them go. Just "be," calling to mind, perhaps, an image of the Holy One and resting in that presence (no prayer requests, no "shoulds" or "oughts," just being present with God). The mandala meditations and the centering prayers provided in this book are intended to assist you in practicing being present to yourself and to the Sacred.

SACRED STORY

Meditation sometimes changes our way of "seeing"—the way we see ourselves, others, and our world. Any image, object, or task, once mundane or even boringly repetitive, may be infused with a sense of the sacred when seen as an invitation to deeper self-exploration or as an opportunity for practicing meditation. Washing the dishes, looking at a flower, standing before a painting, digging a new garden, meeting someone for the first time, listening to an old friend—all afford the opportunity to look deeply at the moment, to see the light or humor or prayerfulness of the experience or the other person. As one's mind and heart become more spacious and more attuned to this contemplative way of being in the world, one's self image changes as well. Loving oneself comes more easily, as does a sense of reverent oneness with creation and with others.

Deborah Anderson's mandala quilt, "Queen Anne's Garden," inspires contemplation. Looking intently at its repetitive images moves one's gaze around the mandala circle and offers delightful surprises along the way—a button here, a vase there, a tile in between. Deborah describes the process of making the mandala with these words:

"The outer border of the quilt is made using the repetitive pattern of a single photograph, taken of a craved stone found at Didiama, Turkey. My computer has the capacity to print an image as it is and to print it in reverse. This 'trick' was employed again with the stack of scarves on either side of the beaded Queen Anne's Lace images.

"Traditional Turkish women wear scarves, hiding their hair. The four-lobed center was made from a single photograph of the corner of a wood block printed scarf. The scarf has *oya* on the edge, a needle-lace.

"The *American Heritage Dictionary of the English Language* defines 'transmogrification' in this way: 'to change into a different shape or form, especially one that is fantastic or bizarre.' In this mandala, I have combined a variety of images to create a totally different meaning. There are flowers from Turkey (ones we call Queen Anne's Lace in the West, which I never expected to see in Turkey, but there they were!), Turkish tiles from a Muslim mosque, and scarves—a traditional garment for Muslim women—each represented in several ways. For me, these inanimate, delightful treasures from Turkey combine to form a circular image of lightness, like fresh spring air, that could bring warmth to any heart."

SACRED MEDITATION

Sacred Text

By meditation upon light and upon radiance, knowledge of the spirit can be reached and peace can be achieved.   —Patanjali, c. 300 B.C.E.[3]

Centering Prayer

In breath: "Awaken in me . . ."
Out breath: ". . . Spirit of Stillness."

Sacred Reflections

What attracts you to meditation?

What meditative practice(s) work for you? What challenges do you encounter?

What might the Holy One be saying to you today about meditation?

Mandala Meditation

Prop Deborah's mandala quilt where you can see it easily. Light your candle. Take several deep, slow breaths (expand your belly, without moving your chest on the in-breaths). Use the preceding centering prayer until you become still. When you are

SACRED QUILT

"Queen Anne's Garden" by Deborah Anderson. From the collection of
Fidelity Investments, Covington, Kentucky. Images created by heat transfers
made from photos taken in Turkey by the artist.

ready, focus your eyes on the mandala's center. Continue your deep breathing as you keep your eyes still. Simply "notice" any distracting thoughts when they arise, and then release them. Keep your focus on the mandala.

When you are ready, close your eyes. Call to mind the mandala and take note of any feelings or images that come to you in the stillness. Simply observe their presence; you can return to them later. Staying in the stillness, open your eyes and gently direct your gaze around the circle of the mandala, noticing images that repeat and ones that seem to capture your attention.

As you end the meditation, give thanks for moments of stillness, for any renewed sense of holy presence, and for the beauty of this mandala quilt.

◦ Circles ◦

s a child, I loved to draw circles. They fascinated me. I could make them any size, fill them with stars or dots or stripes, or leave them open. I could make them loop, spiral, overlap, swirl. Any color or combination of colors fit inside a circle. Made mostly freehand, my circles had no need of compass, protractor, or ruler—although sometimes the precision of the tool-created circles thrilled me. The space beyond the circle offered another playground of design possibilities, space ripe for more shapes, colors, trees, animals—whatever I was "into" at the moment. Sometimes the centers of my circles were mere dots, other times elaborate stars or flowers or concentric rings in radiant colors.

Mostly I kept this circle art to myself, convinced at some level that it was "doodling" unworthy of the granddaughter of an artist. I remember seeing no similar artwork from my siblings or my classmates, but perhaps we were each convinced it was "babyish." Little did I know what a universal symbol I was creating or what a universal pastime engaged my young soul. John O'Donohue, in his book *Anam Cara,* writes about time as a circle and says:

> Deep within the human mind, there is a fascination with the circle because it satisfies some longing within us. It is one of the most universal and ancient shapes in the universe. The earth is a circle; and even time seems to have a circular nature. . . . The year is a circle. . . . This rhythm is even mirrored in the day. . . . First, the new dawn comes out of the darkness, strengthening toward noon, falling away toward evening until night returns again.[1]

Unlike a landscape or a portrait, any circle I drew was complete with the stroke of my pencil or paint brush. The comfort I received from creating circles must have, unconsciously, come from this linkage to the ancient ones and to this universal archetype of wholeness. Decades later, I look back with awe, having come full circle, back "home" to mandalas as a powerful symbol for meditation, healing, and wholeness in my life.

These reflections send me to my bookshelves to retrieve a book by Sue Bender. I remember her writing about a Zen calligrapher and teacher who decorated his walls with bold and audacious circles.

> The circles he draws are called *enso* in the Japanese Buddhist tradition. A Zen circle, Kaz explained, is an expression of enlightenment—"an experience of completeness." Every time it is drawn with a brush it is *unique* for each individual, for each moment.[2]

So, although universal, circles reflect our individual stories, our moments of enlightenment and wisdom, our times of wholeness and health. Bailey Cunningham, author and founder of the Mandala Project, calls circles the "common denominator of human experience."[3] She has experienced how circles and mandalas capture our imagination, embody peacefulness, and open remarkable possibilities for reconnecting us to our past, to our selves, and to the Sacred.

Other circles in my own life come to mind. The quilted candle cloth that marks my morning meditation space is a mandala. The people who gather with me in prayer form a circle. My family and friends encircle my table for meals and card games and celebrations. My favorite quilting hoop is circular. Around a bonfire at camp we sit in a circle for sharing, singing, laughing, praying, and making s'mores. Walking the sweeping arcs of the labyrinth circle brings me back to my center and to God. Whenever I lead workshops, retreats, or worship, I arrange the seating in a circle so that we can all see one another directly and each becomes a part of the whole. Intentionally, as well as unintentionally, I create circle after circle in my life.

SACRED STORY

In describing his own process of creating his mandala quilt, "New Dawn," J. Bruce Wilcox uses these words:

"It is my nature to draw mandalas, and many of my art quilts are designed around a central point. I decided that I not only wanted to create a circular design for this quilt, but I wanted it to spiral as well. Geometry is very sacred to me, as are spirals, so although I had been contemplating this project for a while, it took creating a first drawing that did not work the way I wanted it to, in order to figure out mathematically how to get exactly the result I wanted.

"My design is centered on a nine-pointed star, splitting off into eighteen sections. In the Tarot, the number nine represents the Hermit, the Law of Perfection, while eighteen represents the Moon, the Law of Cycles. After creating the eighteen spokes for my design, I drew equidistant circles out from my center point. Then, because I wanted my design to go from a pointed star in the center to an outside edge with no zigzag, I measured new graded circles on either side of my equidistant circles. Drawing these secondary circles marked all of my points, allowing me to draw in the zigzags. I could then create the spiral by moving over one line with each new line outward from the center.

"The colors for my fabric palette consist of a number of pairs, all with surface metallic print. Several were brand new, while some were a season or two older. Of the two fabrics used for the outside edge, one has a very subtle sun rising or setting through the clouds. I thought it would be very interesting to take this textile, with a very obvious up/down direction to it, and make it spin around my circle. The other fabrics checkerboard into the center, to a starry night print.

"All facets of the creative process are meditative to me. I love to design, make my own patterns, and construct things as well. But my hand quilting is the most meditative, as I sit listening to music while working on my art.

"In coming up with a title for the mandala quilt, I decided that my sun should be rising up out of night, and therefore not be a setting sun, so New Dawn appeared. This piece represents the beginning of the next phase of growth, acceptance, and success of my art . . . and a new day dawning."

SACRED MEDITATION

Sacred Text

And the end of all our exploring
Will be to arrive where we started
And to know the place for the first time.   —T. S. Elliot[4]

Centering Prayer

In breath: "Holy One . . ."
Out breath: ". . . encircle me."

SACRED QUILT

*"New Dawn" by J. Bruce Wilcox. Machine pieced and hand quilted.
Created to mark the completion of one life cycle and the beginning of a
new, more powerful and positive one.*

Sacred Reflections

Where are the circles in your life?

When have times of enlightenment or wholeness or prayer been within a circle?

What circles would you love to create?

Mandala Making

Gather your art supplies and/or fabric around you. Light your candle and rest quietly in its light for a few moments. Breathing deeply, use the preceding centering prayer to come to deeper stillness.

Call to mind memories of the circles of your life. Notice both the colors and the feelings that come with these memories. When you are ready, draw a circle and place in it images of your life's circles. Use the colors of your fabric, pencils, or paints to recreate the colors and feelings of your memories. Continue to create this mandala as you have time. If you keep a journal, write about the feelings you encountered or share them with a friend.

As you continue to create or write, offer thanks to the Holy One for the circles of insight, healing, and enlightenment in your life.

Centering

Journeying to the center of the soul is what meditation is all about. There, at our core, is the essence of the Holy. Indelibly created in the image of God, we carry deep within our very being the constant possibility for connecting to our Creator. Our Quaker brothers and sisters speak of the Light of God within each of us. This image gives rise to another for me — an image of a precious nugget of luminous light deep in my soul and God-given at birth. The God-light within streams its way instantly and mysteriously, whenever uncovered, to connect to the eternal light of the Holy One.

The challenge is to uncover the light, to touch or dwell in the center in ways that keep clear the pathway of connecting radiance. Yet, as wise ones throughout the ages have known, getting to the center can be, and often is, difficult. The path inward can be murky, painful, cluttered, or frightening. Life's hurts have a way of accumulating and intruding. What we find when we venture within may be too scary to even approach. Dottie Moore's quilt "Centering" becomes so captivating and hopeful when this reality is understood. The journey is worth the risks; for at our true center we glimpse the light, the peaceful terrain of all that God wills and creates for us. If we are willing to venture through the muck and discipline ourselves to uncover our soul's center, a sense of being "home," of being whole, of satisfying some ancient, mystical yearning pervades our being. The God-light within connects to the whole, holy light of God.

SACRED STORY

The center of a traditional mandala, one in the Tibetan Buddhist tradition, for example, is very defined and often beautifully elaborate. It is considered the home of a Buddha or a deity. Reaching the center of a Tibetan mandala during meditation means achieving enlightenment. In general, meditation on the medial point of a mandala brings life back to focus and stimulates feelings of centeredness and balance. Quilters have been known to experience those same feelings. "Time and again, women and men who quilt return to their quilt projects for a sense of centering, a time of pulling in all the frazzled fragments of a day and reconnecting with oneself and with God."[1]

In much the same spirit, Dottie Moore talks about her mandala quilt:

"'Centering' was commissioned by a woman challenged with major health issues. Her only request was that the piece be meditative. I knew she liked purple, so I began by painting fabric, holding the woman in my heart, and meditating.

"The river winds like a path through a valley leading toward the mountains. The mountains represent strength and power. They are green, the color of healing and the heart chakra. The trees are expressions of life. The colors of blue and purple were selected to represent the spiritual side of healing. Blue is also the color of the throat chakra and the voice.

"I wrote blessings on small pieces of fabric and stitched them between the layers of the quilt and offered prayers of healing as I stitched.

"After the quilt was completed, I called the woman who commissioned it. She told me that she was halfway through her chemotherapy and that her blood count was already back to normal—she was in remission! Her whole perspective on life had changed. She was positive and fully centered in the present moment. Although some days the chemotherapy made her quite ill and weak to the point of having to stay in bed, she was finding the time and strength to make small quilts to donate to her local hospital."

SACRED QUILT

"Centering" by Dottie Moore. Machine and hand embroidered,
machine quilted. Commissioned as a healing quilt for a woman challenged
with major health issues. Photo by Michael Harrison.

SACRED MEDITATION

Sacred Text

Simplification comes when we "center down," when life is lived with singleness of eye, from a holy Center where the breath and stillness of Eternity are heavy upon us and we are wholly yielding to God. Some of you know this holy, recreating Center of eternal peace and joy and live in it day and night. Some of you may see it over the margin and wistfully long to slip into that amazing Center where the soul is at home with God. Be very faithful to that wistful longing. It is the Eternal Goodness calling you to return Home. —Thomas Kelly, 1941[2]

Centering Prayer

In breath: "Holy One of Light . . ."
Out breath: ". . . fill me with light anew."

Sacred Reflections

When have you experienced being centered in the Holy?

What practices help you to center?

What feelings or memories or dreams do you encounter in your centering process?

Mandala Making

Sit in your favorite posture for meditation, with the picture of Dottie Moore's mandala quilt before you. Ponder it softly with your eyes, starting from the outer edge of the circle, slowly moving ever inward toward the center, and noticing along the way what feelings surface as you move inward.

Close your eyes and ask for an image of your own center. Wait patiently for an image to come. Notice any colors and feelings that accompany your image and hold those in your heart. After you have rested with the image for as long as you desire, sketch the image within a circle, being careful to do so without judgment or inhibitions. Now or later, fill in the image with colors, write about it in your journal, or share its significance with a trusted friend.

As you create or as you journal about your mandala, offer thanks for the sacredness of your own center and for the beauty of the "Centering" quilt.

Journey

he tradition of making pilgrimages to holy places is common to many faiths. Shrines around the world mark experiences of being in the presence of the Divine and great stories abound that capture the joys and tribulations of traveling to sacred lands. The labyrinth was created to simulate the walk when our ancestors were unable to make a pilgrimage journey. Over time, labyrinths themselves—and the places where they were located—became holy sites as well. Located outside of Paris, Our Lady of Chartres Cathedral with its ancient labyrinth, for example, has been a popular pilgrimage site since the Middle Ages.

A frequent pilgrim to Chartres Cathedral, Dr. Lauren Artress describes the labyrinth and its symbolism in these words:

> Labyrinths are usually in the form of a circle, with a meandering but purposeful path to the center and back out again, large enough to be walked into. Each has only one path, and once we make the choice to enter it,

the path becomes a metaphor for our journey through life, sending us to the center of the labyrinth then back out to the edge on the same path.[1]

Our progress through life is often referred to in journey metaphors. Early Christians were known as "People of the Way." The Native American vision quest is an invitation to journey into nature for those seeking the divine truth within. The urge to "find your own path" in life is universal. Both labyrinths and mandalas entice us to move deeply inward toward our own center; our own wisdom. In the process of walking a labyrinth or meditating upon a mandala, as we reach the center, our "soul assignment" may become more clear, healing deep wounds along the way and touching truths about ourselves often unrevealed to us before.

SACRED STORY

Sheila Steers made her labyrinth quilt as an entry in a quilt show in Eugene, Oregon. The show's "challenge category" theme was "Peaceful Reflections." She writes about the quilt with these words:

"I am not sure when the inspiration came to make a labyrinth. Once the thought was there, no other idea seemed as intriguing to me. Here was an ancient and honored means of gaining a sense of peace or reflection. A photograph of the labyrinth of the Cathedral of Chartres in France was my design source.

"In order to maintain a feeling of calm, I chose to work with a limited range of colors. The labyrinth was cut from one piece of hand-dyed fabric and hand-appliquéd to a background containing six circles radiating from light to dark purple. The center petals are a different hand-dyed fabric. The labyrinth circle rests on fabric that reflects its own circular pattern.

"Walking a labyrinth is a peaceful, reflective experience for most people. When one can't walk a large path, smaller 'finger' labyrinths can be used. I walked the path with my needle. After appliquéing the center petals and circle, I chose to appliqué along one side of the path, moving from the center out and then back to the center along the other side. In this way I had a little of the experience of walking the path. Often I would find myself tracing the curves of the fabric with my fingers or eye before putting the piece away for the night.

"Doing the appliqué by hand was a slow process, yet I thought about a lot of things while sewing. In looking back over that time, I remember a general feeling of being relaxed, even when turning under the inside corners (a patience-demanding task even on good days!). I looked forward to doing the appliqué each evening. It became a good way to end the day.

"After so much handwork, the quilting itself was done by sewing machine. The quilting lines give me a second labyrinth on the back of the quilt. This too has been traced by finger and eye. I enjoy the labyrinth's restfulness and the calm feeling I get from a visual and tactile perspective. I plan to make more!"

SACRED QUILT

"Walk With Me" by Sheila Steers. Hand appliquéd and machine quilted.
The first place winner in her guild's 2002 quilt show, the artist created this
mandala to interpret the show's theme: "Peaceful Reflections."

SACRED MEDITATION

Sacred Text

When we are able to take one step peacefully and happily, we are working for the cause of peace and happiness for the whole of humankind. Walking meditation is a wonderful practice.
—Thich Nhat Hanh[2]

Centering Prayer

In breath: "Holy One within . . ."
Out breath: ". . . I circle back to you."

Sacred Reflections

Write in your journal or share with a friend some of the stories of your own sacred journey: your birth or baptism story, early memories of holy places and people in your life, moments of self-discovery or the finding of your "voice," times of finding yourself "on track," times of hope and times of struggle, any of the twists and curves of your life.

Mandala Making

Pray several times the preceding centering prayer, or use one of your own to move into a quiet stillness. With your finger, begin at the small blue circle at the bottom and slowly follow the path of Sheila's labyrinth to the center. Rest in the center. Allow a sense of spaciousness to enfold you there as you listen within for the Holy. Perhaps a word or an image will come to you. If so, offer thanks and hold it in your heart. If not, fear not, simply enjoy the spacious restfulness of coming home to your own center.

When you are ready, follow with your finger the path outward from the center of the labyrinth, gently noticing any feelings or images that come to you. After you are outside the labyrinth again, breathe deeply and rest in quiet stillness. Repeat again the centering prayer.

Now or later, fill a mandala circle with symbols of your own journey inward or create a mandala that moves you to your own sense of centeredness. As you create, offer prayers of thanksgiving for the journey of life that is yours.

Consider taking a meditative walk today, if you are able. Walk slowly, breathing deeply and noticing all of creation.

· D r e a m s ·

he language of the dream world is mystical and whimsical, elusive, yet revelatory, and sometimes hilarious. Dreams are often God's language, a way for the Holy One to break through all of the everyday clutter and chatter of our minds to speak to us from within. Tending to our dreams can be a form of meditation, a way to open to God and to the wisdom and light of God in our own souls.

Carl Jung, the great Swiss psychiatrist, popularized mandalas in the West, although they had been a part of both Eastern and Western religious traditions for thousands of years. He first encountered mandalas in his own dreams. Initially unfamiliar with their symbolism and significance, Jung drew the mandalas of his dreams in his journals and reflected on their meaning in his own life. Research led him to the universality of mandalas and to their archetypal significance as symbols of transformation, wholeness, and integration. Jung found that when his patients were encouraged to create and reflect on mandalas, they moved more assuredly through their depression or fearfulness towards deeper self-knowledge and integration.

Laura J. Watts, in her book *Mandalas*, describes the Native American dream catcher as "a mandala of the dream world."[1] Created within a circular hoop, the dream catcher's spiral web is designed to catch the good dreams and all that they teach, and to let the bad ones pass through. The space in the center of the dream catcher is to allow the dreamer's spirit to pass into the world of dreams, protected from any bad spirits or frightful dreams.

Quilts, too, are connected to our dream world and to the Holy. The creation of an heirloom quilt is a long process, affording frequent times of solitude and meditation. Women and men who quilt often use that solitude to infuse their work with dreams and hopes, prayers and blessings for the recipient. Also, it is not surprising to find that in that solitude, dream fragments return to mind from the previous night. When I have that experience, I immediately set aside my quilting to capture the dream in my journal, if I have not done so already. Often the dream is related to the quilt. My friend Barbara Davis gives a beautiful example of such a dream in this book's chapter entitled "Birth." There is a legend, too, about quilts and dreaming, in which a young woman who sleeps under her quilt for the first time will dream of her beloved. Regardless of the truth or reality of such a legend, the story reflects the countless experiences people have reported over the years of finding warmth, comfort, and healing when wrapped in a quilt or when sleeping under one.

For people new to the symbolism of dreams and personal mandalas, and for suggestions on how to recall and "listen" to dreams, books abound. I recommend the works of Ann Faraday and the book *Dream Work* by Jeremy Taylor. In many places, there are also small groups of folks who share and interpret dreams together. Since dreams are often very revealing, these groups usually form when a few trusted friends come together with the intent of helping one another remember and interpret their dreams. Chapter 8 in Jeremy Taylor's book includes "Twenty-one Basic Hints for Group Dream Work."

SACRED STORY

Often intertwining, dreams, quilts, and mandalas offer metaphors and symbols that lead to self-understanding and to sacred connections. When I am faithful about recording my dreams, when I take time to meditate on the images and messages they bring forth, I often find God "speaking" to me. As I read Beth Ann Williams' reflections on her quilt "Dreamtime," I was fascinated by her meditative process and delighted that she entitled the mandala as she did, hinting that one of the ways we "awaken" is through our dreams. She writes:

"Drawing has always been a safe haven for me, a way of centering myself, calming, a refuge from the chaos of life—whether external or internal. When I became a quilt maker, I discovered that the process of creating a quilt brings me comfort in much the same way. And although I have only recently become aware of the history of mandalas, I recognize that I have been creating mandala quilts for many years, often (but not always) Celtic in style, and using them as an important component in my healing and growth. Not only do the rather mundane, repetitive tasks of cutting and sewing force me to physical discipline and orderliness, but also the design process itself serves to focus my mind and spirit.

"As I move my pencil over the paper, I find myself in a meditative state in which I am released from the often debilitating physical pain of chronic illness and rediscover a sense of self beyond myself, beautiful and whole. Wrapped safely and securely in the arms of my Creator, I am free to release any fear or anxiety and revel in the love and joy of new creation.

"Paradoxically, I often sense that, rather than bringing something totally new into existence, I am merely making visible some truth that already exists—even if only in an inarticulate, shadowy, dreamlike form. When I regard a finished mandala quilt, I am often amazed at the journey embodied in the flowing lines and brilliant colors, light, and shadows. And I am grateful."

SACRED QUILT

"Mandala Series: Dreamtime" by Beth Ann Williams. Invisible machine appliqué and machine quilting with variegated rayon thread. The artist believes that perhaps some pre-existing truth, in dreamlike form, comes through in this quilt.

SACRED MEDITATION

Sacred Text

The soul in sleep gives proof of its divine nature. —Cicero

Centering Prayer

In breath: "Breathe in light and color . . ."
Out breath: ". . . breathe out dimness and gloom."

Sacred Reflections

What has been your experience of remembering dreams?

What symbols, from your dream world or waking world, are sacred to you?

What might the Holy One be saying to you today about dreams and meditation?

Mandala Meditation

Prop Beth Ann's mandala quilt where you can see it easily. Light your candle. Take several slow, deep breaths, noticing the air as it goes in and out. Use the preceding centering prayer.

When you are ready, focus your eyes on the mandala's center. Keeping your eyes as still as possible, continue your deep breathing. Notice and then release any thoughts that may come to you and remain focused on the mandala. When you feel still, close your eyes. Call to mind the mandala, taking note of any feelings or images that come to you now in the stillness. Simply observe their presence; you may return to them later. Imagine the light from the center of the mandala flowing directly into your heart, your spirit. Rest in that light.

As you end the meditation, give thanks for moments of stillness, for any renewed sense of holy presence, and for the colorful beauty of this mandala quilt.

Balance

I crave time by the ocean. My entire being seems to yearn for the rhythm of the waves crashing on the shore and then receding majestically. When I sit alone by the sea, the sounds and sights of nature—of water, of sky, and sand—all conspire to bring the energies of my soul into balance. I don't understand how it happens exactly, and I always experience the awe of those moments as one of the mysteries of God's universe. I can close my eyes and feel the pull of the sea as it rushes back from the sand. I can feel the vibrations of sound wash over me as the crashing waves echo in every cell of my being. Energy begets energy. Then, adding to sounds and sensations, there is the visual symmetry of vast, equal portions of sky and ocean on the horizon and the warm sands of "Mother Earth" beneath my bare feet. Being on this holy ground restores to my soul some long lost equilibrium.

My solitude by the sea happens in early morning, as close to sunrise as I can manage. Frequently, it's just me and the occasional person fishing who are up that early. Especially in those first hours of a summer morning, I assume anyone else on the beach is there following the same yearnings of the soul as I am—kindred spirits, sensing but not having to explain our presence on the shore—except on one occasion, a few years ago. Facing the rising sun, I must have been sitting very still. I did not hear the elderly man approach; rather, I sensed his presence close by and opened my eyes. After a perfunctory comment on the beauty of the sea and the sunrise, he began to closely question me about how I was doing and whether or not I had family and/or friends nearby. My mind was rapidly trying to decide if he was a lecherous, threatening old man or a benevolent, self-appointed "chaplain-by-the-sea." Picking up several fishermen in my peripheral vision, and sensing no immediate danger, my fear began to subside and I suddenly realized he was concerned that I might throw my presumably despondent self into the ocean at any moment. After a few awkward minutes of his questions and my somewhat evasive responses (I was not going to tell him anything specific about my life!), he left. He must have been reassured, to some limited extent, that I was not about to walk into the sea, never to return.

As his figure grew small in the distance, I did a mental inventory: Had I been feeling despondent? Was I projecting a need to be rescued? Was God sending an "angel" to head off a calamity of some nature? I was reasonably certain the answer was "no" to each question. What did occur to me, however, was that I was lonely for someone with whom to share the awe of the sunrise, the wonder of the waves and their rhythm, and the deep sense of peace and balance invoked in my soul just by being there each morning. I was out of balance. I still needed the "with-ness" of a soul-friend. My solitude needed the counterpoint of sharing with a trusted friend the deep waters of my soul. For several weeks prior to this vacation, I had been contemplating seeking out a spiritual director. On the beach that morning, I came to know—perhaps through an angel after all—that it was the "right" time to do so. I resolved to make that connection as soon as I returned home.

Also, the next day, I invited my husband to join me on the beach for morning meditation. Usually not fully awake until sometime after noon and his first cup of coffee, he nevertheless rallied for the sunrise and the need I expressed for his presence in that holy space. Sharing both in silence and in conversation, our relationship deepened in a way it would not have otherwise. Grace upon grace followed the interruption of a "stranger."

SACRED STORY

When we seek balance in our lives, the whole earth is involved. The sea, the seasons, the mountains, valleys, deserts, rivers, lakes, and creatures of the earth—all conspire to connect us and balance our participation in what Chief Seattle called "the web of life." In her book *Pocketful of Miracles,* Joan Borysenko recounts this story from his life:

> In 1854, when Chief Seattle gave up his tribal lands in the Pacific Northwest, he made an impassioned plea for us to be good stewards of the land, to honor the sacredness of life because "all things are interconnected. What befalls the earth befalls the sons and daughters of the earth. We did not weave the web of life; we are merely a strand in it. Whatever we do to the web, we do to ourselves."[1]

Throughout history, many circular symbols, including mandalas, have been employed to represent balance. The yin and yang symbol, for example, has been used for over three thousand years in Chinese culture. With great simplicity, it depicts balance and harmony between *yin*: the moon, darkness, and the feminine, and *yang*: the sun, light, and the masculine. In her quilt "Equinox," Barbara Crane captures our yearning for balance in several ways. She describes her quilted mandala in these words:

"'Equinox' refers to many different balances—the vernal equinox, a time of equal day and night; a visual equilibrium between sky and earth; and the Taoist yin-yang, symbolizing masculine/feminine energies, aggressiveness/receptivity, creativity/dissolution, and other types of balance.

"I loved rummaging through my fabric collection until I discovered each new combination of fabrics to create the light and shadow effect around the yin-yang circle. As I worked, I felt that I must pay complete attention to this effect, which seemed both fragile and powerful. The top was nearly completed when I was startled to discover some sort of large bird—a swan perhaps—emerging from the circle, all of its own accord. This unplanned bird has as its eye the upper small circle; its beak extends toward the right of the quilt. It seemed to me that 'Equinox' had borne perfect fruit: life itself emerged from the balance of the circle."

SACRED QUILT

"Equinox" by Barbara Lydecker Crane. Created to highlight the vernal equinox and the Taoist yin-yang symbol. Unexpected life emerges as a bird head appears in the sky, with a long beak pointing right.

SACRED MEDITATION

Sacred Text

Every part of this soil is sacred in the estimation of my people. Every hillside, every valley, every plain and grove, has been hallowed by some sad or happy event in days long vanished.   —Chief Seattle

Centering Prayer

In breath: "Goddess of the Earth . . ."
Out breath: ". . . ground me in your wisdom."

Sacred Reflections

In what aspects of life do you seek balance or harmony?

What part of nature evokes a sense of balance for you? What people?

When have you experienced moments of balance or harmony? Imbalance?

Mandala Making

Sit or stretch out on the floor for a few moments by your lighted candle. As you take several deep breaths, relax into the stillness. Close your eyes and notice how your body is feeling. Starting at your feet and moving slowly upward, tighten and then relax any points of tension in your body. Again, rest in the stillness. When you are ready, go to the part of your body that is your center and notice the feelings there. Imagine holding those feelings in your hands, then gently setting them aside on a colorful piece of cloth. You will return to them later.

Focused on your center, invite an image or memory of balance in your life. Wait and rest. If an image or a memory comes to you, offer a prayer of thanks and hold the image in your center. When you are ready, draw a circle and create your image or a symbol of your memory within the mandala. If no image came to you, simply begin with the circle and see what comes. Using your fabric or other art supplies, continue to create this mandala as you have time today. Ponder also the learnings, feelings, and insights that come from times when everything seems out of balance. Perhaps those times will be reflected in your mandala. As you create, give thanks for all of life and for the intricate web that holds you and connects you to others and to the world.

Later, remember the feelings that you discovered in your center. Record them in your journal, or speak of them to a trusted friend, noticing which one or ones seem to need your attention. Offer to the Holy One your prayers about these feelings.

Blessing

In 1999, my friend Barb Davis and I began offering a yearly retreat for women based on the book we had just written, *With Sacred Threads: Quilting and the Spiritual Life*. For me, one of the most moving moments of the Sacred Threads Retreats comes at the end of our several days together, during our closing worship. Each quilter coming to the retreat has been invited to bring along a sacred quilt, one that connects to her own spiritual journey in some way. As the final worship draws to a close, we have a "Blessing of the Quilts." We invite each quilter who cares to do so, one by one, to share the story of her quilt. Like each quilter and each quilt, the stories are unique, deeply moving, and profoundly faith-filled. Many stories stand out in my mind: one quilt honored a beloved father-in-law who had died, another celebrated the survival of breast cancer, and another marked a daughter's high school graduation. There have been stories of quilts made by great-grandmothers, a quilt made by several sisters to honor their parents' fiftieth wedding anniversary, and one made in memory of a mother's death. Each story is received with loving acceptance and a large dose of awe. Each story testifies in some way to the artistry, faith, and resilience of a woman's spirit.

After each quilt is placed in the center of our worship circle and its story is told, we say together, "Bless this quilt of love and memories. Bless this quilt and its creator." With these simple words, we dedicate to God both the quilts and the quilt makers, marking them as sacred, their artistry an honor to the one Great Creator.

There are many types of blessings. In Hebrew the word for blessing is *berakah* and blessings are spoken countless times during the day by our Jewish brothers and sisters. Joan Borysenko, author and spiritual mentor, tells about these prayers of gratitude:

> Judaism is similar to Greek Orthodoxy in being a tradition of gratitude. In Judaism there are over a hundred blessings that express our gratitude to God for every kind of natural wonder. . . . The bracha is a blessing of God for all that has been created. You can say an impromptu blessing whenever you notice something of wonder or beauty: *"Blessed art Thou, Creator of the Universe, who has given us the first star of the evening, or the light of the moon, or the smile of babies."*[1]

These blessings, directed to God, are rooted in awe and convey thankfulness for the creative goodness of the Holy One.

Another type of blessing comes from the Christian scriptures, where the word most often translated as "bless" is the Greek word *eulogeo*, meaning "to speak well of" or "to express praise." It is the root of the word "eulogy." Spoken by one person to another, this blessing invokes God's graciousness and power or expresses to God feelings of thankfulness and praise for the person. Sometimes accompanied by the "laying on of hands" or, in baptism for example, the use of water or oil, these blessing rituals seek to infuse God's own spirit and light into the person's life.

For years, I have ended letters and e-mail messages with simple blessing words, such as: "Many Blessings," or "God's Blessings to You," or "Blessings Always." These phrases are my shorthand versions of longer, unwritten blessings, articulated only in my heart: "May the God of Love bless and keep you always" and for the prayer in my heart: "Blessed are you, O Holy One, Creator of the Universe, for you have given me this precious friend . . . this amazing daughter . . . this wondrous person in my life." Writing to someone is indeed a form of prayer, a way of calling to mind the recipient, and those intentional, closing words of blessing are powerful and grace-filled. So much so, that I am inspired to give up the "shorthand version" and offer to those I love the unabridged blessings of my heart!

SACRED STORY

In northern India, Rabgoli ground art is created by women to bring "good fortune and protection to home, family or harvest."[2] These mandala-like decorations are most often done in chalk powder, grain, or flower petals in front of a home or building. However, "as a blessing for the household, sometimes rice flour was used so that insects would feed on it."[3]

While I have discovered little additional information on mandalas that directly speaks of them as blessings, I nevertheless feel confident in doing so. In a multitude of ways, whether they are used for healing, centering, or as an avenue to harmony and peacefulness, mandalas access the Holy and invoke into one's life a deep sense of the Sacred.

In countless ways, quilts, too, are blessings. Receiving a quilt is like being wrapped in prayer and being chosen by graciousness. Making a quilt surrounds one in a riot of colors, endless texture and design possibilities, time to express holy cre-ativity and giftedness—each aspect of which affords a wealth of opportunity for open-ing to grace and sacredness. Time and again quilters speak of the blessings for loved ones that they pray and stitch into their quilts. Dottie Moore describes the process of making "Where Love Abides" and her unique way of adding blessings to her quilts:

This quilt "was created for a couple who own another quilt that I had created several years ago. Since the purchase of their first quilt, they moved to California, started their careers and had their first child, a boy born on a blue moon Halloween. They sent me two pages of writing about mandalas, parenthood, and their connection to my work. They told me of some of the colors in the room where the quilt would hang, and that they wanted their son represented in the quilt in some way as a symbol of creation and new life.

"Jeramy, their son, is in the center of this mandala, represented by the tree. He is both the tree and the blue circle since he was born on a blue moon Halloween. The large tree with its protective branches represents the loving family they are creating. The spirals represent change and growth. The squares provide structure and form for their family.

"The colors, purple and green, were chosen to blend with the space where the quilt will hang; however they are symbolically perfect for this quilt. Purple represents spiritual growth and green is the color of healing and the heart chakra."

"I rewrote the writing that they sent me and placed it on the quilt as surface design. I also wrote blessings on small pieces of fabric and stitched them between the layers of the quilt."

SACRED MEDITATION

Sacred Text

I will make of you a great nation, and I will bless you, and make your name great, so that you will be a blessing. I will bless those who bless you . . . and in you all the families of the earth shall be blessed.
—Genesis 12:2, 3

SACRED QUILT

"Where Love Abides" by Dottie Moore. Appliquéd, hand painted, and hand embroidered, celebrating the birth of a first child. From the collection of Andrew Lohmann and Laurie Schoelkopf. Photo by Michael Harrison.

Centering Prayer

In breath: "Holy God . . ."
Out breath: ". . . bless me."

Sacred Reflections

At what times in your life have you felt blessed?

When have you blessed another?

What signs or rituals of blessing are a part of your faith tradition?

Mandala Meditation

Light your candle and sit comfortably in your sacred space. Prop the picture of Dottie Moore's quilted mandala before you. Close your eyes, breathe deeply, and repeat several times the preceding centering prayer. Hold in your heart a sense of being blessed; rest in that feeling.

When you are ready, focus your gaze on the mandala. Starting on the outer edge, notice the richness of the purple background. Notice any way in which this color seems to touch you. Move your gaze inward to the leaves of the large tree, their restive green color, and the warm brown of the branches. Feel the blessing of these colors and symbols in your soul. Continue to slowly move your gaze inward, noticing the colors and the quilting designs, and any sense of blessing they bring.

Let your gaze linger on the center tree, the blue circle, and the tree's brown trunk. In this center place, let your mind become still. Close your eyes and ask for an image of blessing in your own life. Rest with that image. Notice any colors that appear and how they make you feel. As the blessing image seeps into your soul, offer a *berakah*, "Blessed art thou, Creator of the Universe, who has given me this image of . . ." Or use other words of blessing and thanks that come to you.

As you continue to hold this blessing image in your heart, allow your posture to express receptivity. Try sitting very still, with your arms stretched comfortably before you, palms turned upward towards the heavens. Invite God's blessing on your own life. Imagine God placing in your hands all of the light and grace you will need for this day. Feel the warmth of God's blessing travel up your arms and into your body, into your being. Rest in this posture as long as you desire. As you close this meditation, remain in this same posture a few moments longer. Imagine holding in your outstretched hands all of the people and concerns of your heart. Hold them in the blessing light of the Holy One. Offer them to God's care.

Open your eyes when you are ready. Sketch your blessing image into a mandala or write in your journal about the blessings of your life. Employ Dottie Moore's idea of writing blessings on small pieces of fabric or paper. Place them where you or others will find them this day.

Offer thanks for the blessedness of mandalas and for the beauty of Dottie's quilt.

○ · L i g h t · ○

My morning prayer time each day includes the ritual of lighting a candle. In the darkness of early morning, first the match, then the lighted candle are the only sources of light as I begin to center myself and rest in sacred space. In the quiet stillness of the morning, the candle before me invokes a sense of divine presence and leads me deep into the light of my own soul. An admirer of Quaker wisdom and theology, I join with them in believing that each of us has a "light within," a bit of God's own divine light, implanted in our souls at birth by the Creator. Candle light touches soul light, reflecting through every atom of my being the reality of divine love.

On the mornings when centering eludes me and my mind refuses to rest anywhere, let alone in the Holy, at least there is the candle. Circular and luminous, it stands as a sign of God's presence. No matter how scattered or desert-bound my soul feels, that radiant witness to God's continued "with-ness" in my life shines forth. Light is enough, sometimes.

Mandalas, too, are known to be sources of light and enlightenment, connectors to the Divine, illuminators of our deepest selves and amplifiers of the light within. God is often symbolized as light or known as the Light. Enlightenment, too, is frequently depicted by light. Just think about a cartoon character, coming to some insight, with a light bulb going on above his or her head. Creating a mandala may lead to such moments, or celebrate such moments. Meditating on a mandala may reveal light buried deep within one's soul or wisdom waiting to be acknowledged.

In her beautiful and inspiring book *Mandala: Luminous Symbols for Healing*, Dr. Judith Cornell explores in depth the many intricate connections between light, sound, consciousness, and mandalas. Teaching meditation and drawing techniques for creating luminous mandalas, Dr. Cornell assists people in accessing their soul's inner light. That light, depicted within a mandala, offers dramatic possibilities for healing and wholeness—with creation, with others, and within oneself. From ancient mystics to modern-day monks, people have employed mandalas to come to enlightenment and Holy Light, capturing the sacredness of circular symbols in our lives.

A few years ago, believing in the marvel of mandalas, I invited a group of youth to learn about mandalas. During an extended period of silence, the young people were free to create their own mandala, color one from a mandala coloring book, or in some other way express their prayers and reflections on the mandala. Their creations were astounding and spirit-filled. One young woman put pen to paper not to draw, but to offer the following poetic expression of her own giftedness:

MANDALA

Here I am, somewhere inside this circle—
Of faith, of Spirit, of life, of breath.
It encloses me, it finds me, it centers me, it guides me,
And yet, I am lost.
I am the gravitational center of this circle,
And yet, without me, its eternal edge will not be broken.
I am the life-force of this circle,
And yet, it lived before me. It will live after me.
Or have I always been here?
Was I grafted into the root of Eternity?
And when my flower has withered, will I fall to the dust,
And give my strength to another center, another circle?
My un-fenced existence began before the stars,
Before the breath of Dawn,
Before the Whispers of Darkness.
My circle is a simple thought,
Dreamt by God, on God's pillow of righteousness and goodness.
I am cradled by this dream,
And driven by this dream,
And bound to this dream.
And though I am lost within it,
My comfort is
I am Within it.[1]

As I listened to her read her poem to the group and watched the radiance on her face, words of sacred Christian scripture echoed suddenly in my heart: "You are the light of the world . . . let your light shine before others, so that they may see your good works and give glory to your Creator in heaven" (Matt. 5:14–16).

SACRED STORY

Patterns of light and dark are crucial in quilt blocks and quilts. Without variations in the value of the colors, the intricate patterns of the quilt would be lost. Quilters who gravitate towards the warmer, darker colors (and I am one who does) tend to need reminders to choose fabrics from the lighter spectrum of the rainbow. When I have the courage to do so, the effect is often striking. Lighter colors add sparkle and brightness to a quilt. Each time I venture out of my comfort zone of warm hues, I notice my spirit lightens a bit as well. The combination of working with the brighter colors, as well as exercising my creative energies, gladdens my heart, drawing me closer to the Light Within.

As soon as I saw Larkin Van Horn's quilt, I thought of my morning meditation candle. She writes about the process of creating her quilt with these words:

"After reading the mandala making exercise, I had the feeling that this process was going to be very foreign to me. But I was determined to give it an honest try. After two weeks of reading and sketching and thinking and moving fabric around, I was no closer to starting a quilt than I had been at the beginning. I decided this project was not for me, and I was all set to write to Susan, backing out of my commitment.

"A little time passed, and one morning I awoke with the phrase 'reach out in the darkness, and you will find a friend' running through my head. I recognized it as a fragment from an old rock and roll song, but couldn't recall the rest. I wandered into the studio, and an hour later I had laid out a fabric collage of a bright turquoise circle on a dark background. Within a few moments, a glittering cross was in place on top of the circle. Was this a mandala? There was the circle—a symbol of eternity—with another symbol of our Eternal Friend. I was intrigued, so I quilted it and set it aside.

"Again, time passed, and I was still unsure of my participation in the project. I kept seeing circles, but was not moved to work with wedges or curves. Then it happened again. This time I knew the whole song. It was 'Light One Candle' and is about the candles on a menorah. Before long I had another bright circle on a dark background. This time the symbol was a candle, a representation for me of the Trinity: the wax for Christ, the flame for the Creator, and the heat for the Holy Spirit. As I machine quilted, fragments of Bible verses bombarded me: 'And God said, Let there be light; and there was light. And God saw the light, that it was good . . .' (Gen. 1:3).

"These pieces were about moving out of darkness and into the light. They were reminding me about my dependence on God's grace and great mercy. They were about raising my spirits and moving beyond the disappointments of life."

SACRED MEDITATION

Sacred Text

You are the light of the world . . . let your light shine before others . . .   —Matthew 5:14, 16

Centering Prayer

In breath: "God of Radiance . . ."
Out breath: ". . . shine in my soul this day."

Sacred Reflections

What symbol or image would you use to depict light?

How or when have you experienced enlightenment?

How or when have you experienced "desert times" or times without light?

SACRED QUILT

*"Light One Candle" by Larkin Van Horn. Fabric collage and
machine embroidered. A meditation on moving out of the darkness,
into the light, and resting in God. Photo by Mark Frey.*

Mandala Making

Light a candle in your meditation space. Gather around you colorful art supplies: fabric, construction paper, pencils, watercolors—whatever seems to call to you. When you are ready, sit comfortably with the candle before you.

Close your eyes and breathe deeply several times, or for as long as you need. Open your eyes only partially, staring softly at the candle. Invite the Holy One to remind you of a moment of enlightenment from your past, or ask for enlightenment about a present concern in your life. Imagine holding the request on the palm of your hand. Extend your hand toward the candle, holding the request in God's light. After a moment or two, return your hand to a comfortable position and rest quietly in the light of the candle. Imagine Holy light washing over you. Rest some more. If enlightenment or a memory comes to you, give thanks. If not, fear not—you have begun the waiting and seeking for God's light. Notice the colors around you, around your candle, or around your memory. Ponder, then create an image of light or enlightenment within a circle. Work on it as you have time today.

As you create, give thanks for the gift of light to you and to the world.

· Shelter ·

n the tradition of mandalas, the center point is known to be "the most intense expression of the divine . . . the most concentrated experience of the sacred."[1] Called "the palace" in Nepalese Buddhism, the center is understood to actually house the deity to whom the mandala is dedicated.[2] Tibetan monks, creators of colorful and intricate sand mandalas, come to know the designs so well in their minds that they are able to imagine a walk through each level of the palace. This meditative practice culminates with the monk's arrival at the center of the palace, where the Buddha resides and new enlightenment awaits.

Like the mandala, the tree of life symbol has permeated the art and mythology of countless cultures throughout history. Found in the Garden of Eden (as a part of a matched pair with the Tree of Knowledge), connected to eternity (as in ancient Egyptian art), sacramentalized in ritual (as in the Jewish menorah), and cast in timeless monuments (as in Assyria), the tree of life whispers life-giving holiness across the ages. Its symbolism speaks of creation, of growth and fruitfulness, of nourishment and radiant, sheltering protection, of eternal life, certain blessing, harmony between heaven and earth, and of rootedness, wholeness, and health.

With such rich significance and meaning, it is not surprising that the tree has been considered sacred. Because a tree extends into the soil, is "present" above the earth, and also reaches into the heavens, it is often seen as an expression of one's connection to the Holy. Carl Jung felt that "the tree symbolized the urge in each of us to grow and fulfill an inner image of wholeness that mirrors the perfection of God."[3]

So the appearance of trees in the center of several of the mandalas in this book seems in keeping with the ages. The glowing background in Colleen Curry's tree mandala captivates me, delights my yearning for light and color. The tree itself seems gentle and somehow whimsical, as if it strives to offer us a friendly caricature of the great Tree of Life. "Come. Sit in the shelter of my branches," it beckons. " Hug me! Laugh a little. Breathe! In the quiet canopy of my shade is rest, laughter, and new life." The Goddess at the Center calls us into this mandala of shelter and healing.

SACRED STORY

"With my family, I live in a city, but I am adamant about having a home where trees also reside. 'My tree,' however, in not one of the several in our yard, rather one found in the Park of Roses near our home. She's an enormous oak who just 'claimed' me one day. The claiming happened on one of my daily walks with our two dogs, during a time of high stress and low-grade depression. My spirits, which were so without hope that day, collided with her Spirit, which seemed so strong. One minute I was walking and despair-filled, the next minute I was leaning into her strength. My back fit perfectly into a wide crevice in her trunk. Comfort seemed to flow from her bark, through my skin, and into every cell of my body. The intricate web of connection between humankind and creation came alive in my soul. For a little while that day, she and I were one creation. Her roots, deep and anchored in centuries of soil, grounded me in sacredness, and reminded me of my own roots. Her branches, reaching out and heavenward, with leaves gently fluttering in the breeze like thousands of tiny prayer flags, carried my sorrows to the Holy One.

"Many times since, I have left the path just to stand in her shade, to touch or lean into her Spirit, to feel again my life shift back to center. Sometimes I bring home a leaf she has dropped, an acorn, or a bit of dark bark. Each gift makes its way to a noticeable spot in our home, to my dresser, or the window ledge above the sink, or onto the circle of my prayer cloth. Like a talisman, then, whenever I see part of the oak tree, I am aware of her presence, just a few blocks away, and I remember the leaning, the grounding, and the re-centering strength."

SACRED QUILT

"Tree" by Colleen Curry. Machine appliquéd and quilted.
Some leaves are silk; background leaves are painted. Suspended in an
old bass drum hoop, painted blue to represent the sky.

SACRED MEDITATION

Sacred Text

On either side of the river is the tree of life...and the leaves of the tree are for the healing of the nations. —Revelation 22:2

Centering Prayer

In breath: "Strong, Holy, Grounded One . . ."
Out breath: ". . . root me in your love today."

Sacred Reflections

Where have you encountered a tree of life symbol?

What experiences help you to feel rooted in the Holy? Connected to creation?

What symbols depict life or wholeness or holiness for you?

Mandala Making

Sit quietly with Colleen Curry's "Tree" before you, noticing its leaves, then its bark, next its roots, and the earth and grass around them. Notice the feelings the tree evokes in you, the prayers. Close your eyes and invite an image of God before you. Rest in God; center yourself in God's presence. Offer no words; expect none; simply be in God's presence. Breathe deeply. Imagine yourself under the shelter of a tree. Rest there.

When you are ready, draw a circle. Inside of that circle, draw concentric circles, as in the rings of a tree, until you are near to the center. In the center, draw a tree of life, or another image of the Holy that is sacred to you. If you choose, fill in the mandala with colors that are healing and comforting. Place your mandala in a location where you will notice it later.

As you end your meditation, offer prayers of thanksgiving for trees, for shelter, and for all of creation. Consider walking in a park, in the woods, or on a tree-lined street—whatever is available to you today. Notice the majesty and grace trees offer. Be open to being "called" or "claimed" by a tree, if not today, then on another walk or another day.

⦿ Creation ⦿

I was antsy. I had been inside all day, and the day had been glorious — one of those spring days that makes you want to skip like a child and shout with unbridled joy. Discipline prevailed, however, and I maintained my writing schedule like a dutiful daughter of the word — until early evening, at least. Then I could stand being indoors no longer. I put on my tennis shoes, which was the first signal to our dogs that a walk was in store. They bounced with jubilation! Their leashes strained against their excitement as we made our way out the door and down the driveway. As we turned westward, toward the park, I gasped — the sunset was stunning. Brilliant, fluorescent pinks and luminous whites filled an azure sky. Deep purple-grays along the horizon marked the distant tree line towards which we were headed. I stood for several long minutes just taking in the beauty before me. Then the dogs, blatantly unimpressed by the divine artistry in the sky, succeeded in pulling me onward down the sidewalk. As they dashed back and forth to the fullest extent of their leashes, I kept my eyes on the constantly changing sunset, knowing without a doubt why I had been called out into the evening.

Human beings have been mesmerized by creation since the beginning of time. Our connections to the cosmos and to "Mother Earth" have been celebrated in story and song, ritual and symbol in most religious traditions around the world. Ancient people, tillers of the land and keen observers of the skies, were intimately tied to the seasons, to the cycles of the moon and the movement of the sun and stars. They marked time with celebrations and vigils for each solstice and equinox. Even today, many of our most sacred days of celebration—Hanukkah, Easter, Christmas—are linked to both the lunar and solar calendars. Creatures of creation—birds of the air, two- and four-legged animals of land, and countless swimmers of the sea—all have been depicted in art, part of the reverence of life and environment.

Today, in North America, our connections to the earth are frayed and tenuous, our reverence for creation too often overshadowed by economic and technological "needs." I am afraid that our greed and consumerism have often removed from our awareness the effect of our lifestyles on the planet and its people. The spiritual impact of our negligence runs deep, as we end up yearning for an inner peace that is not possible without reconciliation with creation. In his book *Peace Is Every Step*, Thich Nhat Hanh, peace activist and Buddhist monk, makes the following observation:

> Nature is our mother. Because we live cut off from her, we get sick. . . .
> That is why we need to go out from time to time and be in nature. It is
> very important. We and our children should be in touch again with
> Mother Earth.[1]

SACRED STORY

Mandalas have always been closely identified with the cosmos. Many elements of nature are circular and mandala-like. Think of the cells of our bodies, the iris of our eyes, the rings of a tree, ripples on a lake, rings around the moon and Saturn, snowflakes, and flowers. Beyond these actual, natural mandalas, mandalas have grounded and centered the earth's people, symbolically reminding us of the awesomeness of God and of God's creation, as well as our place in that creation.

In many cultures, ancient and modern, the universe has been depicted as a series of concentric rings. In Thames and Hudson's book *Sacred Symbols: Mandala*, these concentric circles are called the "cosmic mandala," and the symbol is described in this way:

> The mandala can be seen as an evocation of the universe, of galaxies swirling around a centre, of planets revolving around the sun. At the same time, it is a model of the soul's journey from the periphery to the centre of all understanding. . . . The mandala is both a universal symbol and a symbol of the universe. . . it is also the essential plan of the whole universe, balancing centrifugal and centripetal forces, combining beginning and end. It is the ultimate symbol of wholeness; its center is unity. . . ."[2]

Echoing these words of universality, Terry Grant describes her quilt, "Earth, Sun, and Moon":

"This is the third quilt I have made employing circular motifs. At first I didn't think of these as mandalas, but as I worked, I realized that is exactly what they are.

"The design begins on the computer, where the wonders of technology allow me to create a shape, then re-create it infinitely, rotating each precisely. While some may not think of such a mechanical process as being contemplative, I find the process quite magical as shapes combine and overlap and create new shapes before my eyes. After printing the outline to size, I begin to pull fabrics that speak to the design. There is no preconceived color scheme or look I am going for and I work from the center of the circle outward, letting the fabric choose its place in the design.

"Over and over I am drawn to the circle as a motif. It represents, to me, wholeness and renewal in life. The earth follows its circular paths and renews itself daily and seasonally. I feel myself circling through life touching the same points over and over—family, art, nature, friends, work. The circle is infinite and unbroken and like earth's gravity, the center irresistibly pulls all the parts toward itself. Like the earth, moon, and sun, we are all traveling in our own orbit, and at the same time tracing increasingly larger circles in the universe."

SACRED QUILT

"Earth, Sun, and Moon" by Terry Grant.
Fused appliqué and machine quilted. Represents how we each travel
in creation, in our own orbits, like the earth, sun, and moon.

SACRED MEDITATION

Sacred Text

The earth is God's and all that is in it, the world, and those who live in it . . . —Psalm 24:1a

Centering Prayer

In breath: "Creator of the Universe . . ."
Out breath: ". . . encircle me."

Sacred Reflections

What part of creation inspires a sense of the Holy for you?

When was a time that you felt connected to the universe?

What daily practices connect you to the earth? To the creatures of the earth?

Mandala Meditation

Light your candle and sit comfortably in your sacred space. Prop the picture of Terry's mandala before you. Breathe deeply, being conscious of each breath in and each breath out as you rest your gaze on the mandala.

When you are ready, close your eyes, continue breathing deeply, and repeat several times the preceding centering prayer. Hold in your heart a sense of being encircled by God. Rest in that feeling. When you are ready to open your eyes, gaze again at the mandalas on the quilt. Notice the colors, the patterns, the feelings they evoke. Pick one of the mandalas and let your gaze rest in its center. Let your mind become still. Close your eyes and ask the Holy One for an image of creation. Rest with that image. Invite the image of creation into your body-center, and anchor it there by placing one hand over it. Open your eyes when you are ready. Sketch or journal about the image that came. If the image fades or becomes elusive, place your hand on your center and recall the symbol you anchored there.

As you end your meditation, offer thanks for the blessings of the universe and for the beauty of this quilt.

◦ **P e a c e** ◦

Peace is elusive. In the culture of the United States, life is often hectic. We continue to value "doing" and busyness as a measure of our lives. Most of us are hard-pressed to name someone we know personally whose external nature and lifestyle would be described as peaceful. Beyond our individual selves, as a nation, peace often seems a low priority in the United States. We remain far removed from peacemaking imperatives such as this one offered by William Sloan Coffin: "Above all, and at almost any risk, we must get the world beyond war. It is not enough to wish for peace, we have to will it, to pray, think, struggle for peace as if the whole world depended upon it, as indeed it does."[1] Instead, as I write, our country has initiated a war with Iraq, furthering the perception that we, as a culture, are a violent people. Our flag has become a symbol synonymous with a brand of patriotism that supports unconditionally our government's war operations and antiterrorist efforts.

In contrast, mandalas breathe peace. Long understood as symbols of wholeness, they invite us into the health and healing that can be found by uncovering our own inner peacefulness. In her wonderful book *Inner Peace for Busy People*, Joan Borysenko reminds us that an "inner radiance of peace and joy is our birthright, our own true nature." We can, she believes, "learn how to come back home to ourselves," to our own center of peaceful being, and to "holy moments of presence."[2] In those moments of presence, she declares, we are helped to discover the "solidarity with life that is the very essence of inner peace."[3]

Over the centuries, mandalas have aided in that process of being present to life—our own and the planet's—and of coming home to peacefulness within ourselves. In the forward to Baily Cunningham's book *Mandala: Journey to the Center*, Dr. Brigitte Spillmann-Jenny writes:

> Experience has shown that people in all cultures and religions feel drawn to (a mandala's) wholeness, especially in times of personal crisis, disorientation, or seemingly unsolvable conflicts. Mandalas provide a sense of inner peace and reconciliation, of order amidst chaos. Meditation and concentration on the mandala's nucleus—a calm, unified center—help to ground people who are in turmoil.[4]

SACRED STORY

Quilt artist Susan Nash tells about her mandala quilt:

"I decided to make a mandala quilt to use as a focal point for my meditation and yoga practice. I chose the Sanskrit symbol for 'om' as the center. 'Om' is the universal sound of peace, of the Divine, and of the universe breathing.

"While making this quilt, I had very extensive foot surgery and was unable to do my yoga, let alone anything else — I was chair-bound! While recovering, my work on this quilt became a very 'centering' experience. It gave me peace in a hectic household where I could no longer do my home and family care. It gave me a sense of patience and well-being. With each stitch, I felt that, in time, I would heal.

"Perhaps any quilt would have had this healing effect on me. However, I like the fact that when I am able to return to my normal life, I will have this quilt to sit in front of during meditation. As I sit before it each day, I know I will continue to find peace, serenity, and grace."

SACRED MEDITATION

Sacred Text

God calls humanity to join as partners in creating
a future free from want or fear, life's goodness celebrating.
That new world beckons from afar, invites our shared endeavor,
that all may have abundant life and peace endure forever.
— "We Cannot Own the Sunlit Sky," a hymn by Ruth Duck[5]

Centering Prayer

As you still and center yourself, breathe in deeply. On each out breath, say aloud the sound "om," slowly and meditatively drawing out the sound of each letter: "oooommmm." Repeat this practice several times. Notice the parts of your body that resonate with the sound. Imagine the vibrations of the sound moving out from you in waves and filling the room, the house, the world with peace.

If the "om" prayer is disquieting, or as an ending to that prayer, you might use the following prayer:

In breath: "God of the Present . . ."
Out breath: ". . . fill me with your peace."

SACRED QUILT

"Om — The Sound of Peace" by Susan Nash.
Machine pieced, hand appliquéd, and intricately hand beaded.
Dye-discharge used to create center symbol.

Sacred Reflections

When have you had an experience of being present—perhaps to another person, to a piece of art, to an experience of nature, or absorption in a project?

What helps you to feel the interconnectedness of all creation?

How do you experience peace within yourself? Within the world?

Mandala Making

With your favorite art supplies gathered around you, take a few moments to be still. Close your eyes and breathe deeply several times. Call to mind an experience of deep peacefulness. Rest in that experience, gently noticing any colors, feelings, surroundings, and sounds that are present in the memory. Invite a symbol or image of this memory of peace and hold it in your heart.

After you have rested with the image for as long as you desire, draw a circle. Fill the circle with one of the colors of peace from your memory. Add your symbol of peace in the center of this mandala. Outside of the mandala, add a background of colors and symbols that speak to you of peace and presence. Recite blessing prayers over your mandala as you create, prayers of thanksgiving for the peace you find in your own life and the peace you dream of for the world.

If you have time today and choose to do so, create another peace mandala. This time, imagine an antagonist in your life, a situation of conflict, or a place of injustice in our world. Turning again to the picture of Susan Nash's quilt, imagine placing this person or place of lack of peacefulness in the mandala's center. Imagine what may be going on inside of this person or situation today. Notice what is going on inside of yourself as you consider this image. Place on yourself no pressure for "resolving" or "forgiving" this person or situation, simply imagine sending holy light and peace into the mandala's center, encompassing all that is held there. Imagine the vibrations of "om," the sounds and songs of peace, flooding the center, the person, the circumstance. Imagine that something shifts, changes, renews. Notice if this shift happens in the mandala, the person, or in yourself.

Create a mandala that reflects this meditation. Use colors or fabrics that come to you, perhaps representing chaos, or perhaps speaking of transformation, understanding, or compassion.

Later in the day, sit comfortably with your peace mandala(s) before you. Be present only to God as you offer your creation(s) as a visual, circular prayer for peace.

• Healing •

 am not an expert on healing, although I have had my share of pain. Most of us have areas of woundedness in our lives. Some wounds are deeper than others, some closer to being healed than others, some physical, some emotional, some wounds not even named yet, perhaps. Knowing that each person I meet has areas of pain in his or her life, I try to be open and tender with the gift of each one's presence. Likewise, I try to be open and tender with each story as I come to know it. This is my goal, at least, even though I succeed at it less than I would like. Nevertheless, I keep trying. As a spiritual director, I am constantly in awe of the way God works in people's lives, steadily, powerfully calling each one to be who we're created to be, supporting each one on the journey towards greater health and healing and wholeness. Not a proponent of the "God never gives us more than we can bear" theology, I have seen *life* give someone more than it would appear she or he could possibly bear. Yet, I have also seen when God, like a whisper on the winds of deepest knowing, has swept through a soul with compassion and unending consolation—even in the midst of terror or tumult: "You can do it. I am here." Healing, usually not instantaneous, nevertheless becomes rooted for the "long haul" in that divine presence and comfort.

Pastors and spiritual directors, doctors and therapists, best friends and closest family members—all are called to stay the course of that long haul towards healing in the lives of another. If you are human, you undoubtedly have someone in your life depending on your presence and compassion in his or her healing process; in fact, there are probably more such people than you know about. Directly or indirectly, each one of us, as a person of faith, witnesses to others a quiet testimony of God's presence, God's "with-ness" in all the muck of life. Each of us, too, receives from others that faithful witness in ways that work gentle healing in our lives. Seldom talked about and rarely tapped into, there is nevertheless a healing energy that encircles us, flows through and into us; connecting us to God, to others, and to ourselves.

Besides that interpersonal, if somewhat subliminal healing energy, we also have the option of intentionally working on our own healing. At various points in our lives, often when the pain is intense or a new life stage brings us back around again to another facet of the wound, we choose to give it significant time and attention. Here are some of the words of wisdom I have gleaned from the experience of others and from my own experience about how one might purposefully attend to healing:

- Speak of it. Seek out a trusted friend and/or a professional counselor, pastor, or support group.

- Do your inner work. Call on and get to know your "true self," journal about the pain, pray about it, and name whatever you are currently feeling about the wound, why you think it is surfacing or resurfacing now, how it is touching other areas of your life.

- Be in community. Go to church or synagogue, surround yourself with the people from whom you might receive healing energy, spoken or unspoken.

- Face the fear. Face it all the way down to the "ground of our being," as Tillich described God, because, as Parker Palmer writes, "the way to God is not up but down."[1]

- Immerse yourself in art, music, dance, or some other creative form of self-expression. Let your creative self out; do your own artwork or go to a museum.

- Remember to laugh. Life and pain can be serious, but there is much evidence that we all need humor, especially in the healing process.

- Take courage. You are not alone; remember that "You can do it. I am here," says the divine whisper. The hard reality and the paradoxical blessing is that we often meet God face to face in the midst of our deepest pain.

- Let it go. If all else fails, take a break from "working on it," and promise yourself you'll come back to it later. You will.

SACRED STORY

Both the making of quilts and the making of mandalas help us draw on the healing energy in our lives. Both also offer an avenue for intentionally tending to our own healing. Authors of books on mandalas frequently include stories of how Carl Jung used mandalas in his own life and in his therapy with others as an expression of the self and a source of healing. Judith Cornell in *Mandala: Luminous Symbols for Healing* shares several powerful stories about the healing effect mandalas can have, and Sheila Finklestein in her work *Magic Quilted Mandalas* offers this quotation:

> The mandala is an ancient structure that supports harmony and balance. We can use its principles within our life and in our relations with nature.

. . . Nourished by beauty, we can recover balance and openness. Once we heal the human heart, we will be empowered to heal the planet.[2]

In our book *With Sacred Threads,* Barb Davis and I share some of the many stories connecting quilts and healing that we received from quilters across our nation. Gail Ferrick's story about making her mandala quilt "Solstice" is another one of those wonderful stories and hints at many of the connections between quilting and healing. She tells about her creation with these words:

"This is an extraordinarily personal quilt that I have rarely shown. I started it before the death of my beloved, Ken, and it was the first piece I was able to work with as I discovered a new life without him. It took on a life of its own and changed dramatically from its original rigidity and literally moved out of the darkness into the light. The piece was the beginning of the rest of my life and is a tribute to a wonderful and loving friend who will forever live in my heart."

SACRED QUILT

"Solstice" by Gail Ferrick.
Created to honor the artist's beloved and to mark
the beginning of the rest of her life.

SACRED MEDITATION

Sacred Text

And God will be with them; God will wipe every tear from their eyes . . . —Revelation 21:3, 4

Centering Prayer

In breath: "Holy, Healing One . . ."
Out breath: ". . . wipe my tears away."

Sacred Reflections

Who provides a healing presence in your life? What place offers a healing environment?

What art form brings you healing?

What in your life most needs healing today?

Mandala Making

Gather your colorful art supplies or fabric into your sacred space. Light your candle and sit comfortably before it. Breathe deeply several times and focus your gaze on Gail's quilt. Notice its colors, its many circles, its connections to nature, the way the circles are contained in the square.

When you are ready, close your eyes and remember the quilted mandala. Rest with the memory a few moments. Invite the Holy One to remind you of a time of healing in your life. What colors, images, or feelings do you associate with that time?

If you desire, invite an awareness of a place that needs healing in your life today. If one comes, hold the awareness gently, noticing your feelings. Imagine placing that awareness, those feelings into a basket and offering them to the Holy One, who will hold and examine them with you. Imagine a symbol of healing or a place in nature that provides healing energy for you.

When you are ready, open your eyes and create a mandala of healing symbols. Offer thanks for the times of healing and for the courage to heal, for the seasons, and all that connects us to creation.

◦ P r e s e n c e ◦

hich Nhat Hanh, in his book *Peace Is Every Step,* has a chapter entitled "Flower Insights." In this chapter, he tells a well known Zen story about a flower, then shares his own reflections on the story and a poem. As I was contemplating Anne Gailhbaud's pretty dahlia quilt and the challenge of being present to my own life, some of Hanh's words and the poem came to mind, and so I share them:

> When someone holds up a flower and shows it to you, he wants you to see it. If you keep thinking, you miss the flower. The person who was not thinking, who was just herself, was able to encounter the flower in depth, and smiled. That is the problem of life. If we are not fully ourselves, truly in the present moment, we miss everything.
>
> I would like to share a poem with you, written by a friend of mine who died at the age of twenty-eight in Saigon . . . "You" refers to a flower, a dahlia.

Standing quietly by the fence,
you smile your wondrous smile.
I am speechless, and my senses are filled
by the sounds of your beautiful song,
beginningless and endless.
I bow deeply to you.[1]

What an incredible way of seeing! The spiritual practice of presence or mindfulness is like that, an experience of bringing all of oneself to the moment and looking deeply. In my own life, those moments when I am truly myself and totally present are fleeting, but they do happen. My yearning is to encounter more of those moments, to discipline myself and practice true presence as often as possible.

How does that work exactly? Partially with intentionality, I think, and partially with mystery. Mindfulness happens, for example, when I look at a dahlia—quilted or actual—and really bring all of myself to the moment of seeing it, intentionally savoring its colors and shape, noticing its "smile," appreciating its place in the garden, its fragrance, its movement; when I see it, deep in my soul, as a gift from the Creator. I lose mindfulness when I begin to get anxious about how the flower needs water or weeding, when I think ahead to how it will look on my table, how dinner needs to be made for the same table and groceries bought, and when I begin to worry about all that needs to be fit into the rest of the evening. Distractions can be plentiful and can easily chase away mindfulness.

Mysteriously, there are moments in life when mindfulness just comes to me, when I am truly myself and truly present to my life at that moment. And, mysteriously, there are also times when it suddenly dawns on me that I could practice mindfulness immediately—while I listen to my friend, or wash the dishes, or plant a flower, or eat an apple. Thich Nhat Hanh concludes his chapter "Flower Insights" with these helpful words: "The secret of the success is that you are really yourself, and when you are really yourself, you can encounter life in the present moment."[2]

May it be so for each of us.

SACRED STORY

Many aspects of creating a mandala or meditating upon one offer opportunity for presence and for being wholly oneself. When I am drawing or painting a mandala, there is no one to impress; it is just for myself, expressive of myself. When I am creating a mandala quilt, I keep before me the same intention: to create it as an expression of my inner self, not as a possible entry into a quilt show of the future. With that intentionality, I can be present to each step of the process and to each design or symbol that emerges.

Certainly there are many repetitive parts of quilt making or mandala making that can be gloriously mindless, allowing me to reflect on my day, ponder a problem, sing, or even talk on the phone. Adding the same detail in the same color to eight or sixteen (or more!) wedges of a mandala can be a mindless activity, as can cutting countless triangles for a quilt, or piecing the same square design three dozen times, or stitching the same swirling pattern in row after row after row of quilting. There are times in my life when I need mindlessness. Yet there are also times when I need to utilize those same repetitive processes as an opportunity to practice presence or the discipline of prayer. Many forms of prayer are based on repetition (mantras, the rosary, litanies) and each act of adding color to a mandala or another triangle to a quilt can be a moment of prayer or blessing.

Whatever process I use for making a mandala, whether on paper or with fabric, whether repetitive or not, I can bring to it my true self and my full presence. Looking at the fabric, I can marvel at color and weave, texture and design. In the fabric, I can see the many people who labor to bring fabric to my home: those who grow and harvest cotton, those who produce dye and apply it so artfully, those who design the patterns on the fabric, those who print the designs, make them colorfast, those who measure the great lengths of each fabric and wrap it around bolts, those who sell, deliver, and stock on shelves those fabric bolts, and so on . . . The same is true of creating a mandala on paper, with colored pencils or watercolors, pastels or oils. Each act of mindfully appreciating those who have helped to bring me to my own creativity is a prayer of thanksgiving, a prayer of blessing. Even without knowing their names, I can offer to God my deep gratitude for each of their contributions to my mandala, my life.

In a similar way, Anne Gailhbaud's creation of her dahlia quilt was an act of mindfulness. Her mother, with whom she was very close, had recently died. Anne's intention was to remember her mother in a place she loved best, her garden. An avid flower grower, Anne's mother would forever be "the queen of the dahlias."

"This dahlia quilt hangs on the wall of my mother's house. She is not there, but it is not possible for me to take down the quilt. My mother is there in spirit. She had a beautiful garden near a charming river, and her specialty was dahlias, in an incredible collection of forms and colors. Autumn in her garden was wonderful! So, I always sew a dahlia, leaving a background space between the flower and the provincial borders, making the dahlia seem like the rose window of a gothic cathedral. Each stitch of this quilt brought to mind my mother, including the intricate quilting stitches in the black background. My mother is dead, but I still have her quilt. For me, the quilt is like a crown, a crown for the queen of the dahlias."

SACRED QUILT

"Dahlia" by Anne Gailhbaud.
Created to honor the artist's mother,
the "queen of the dahlias."

SACRED MEDITATION

Sacred Text

For the human heart and mind are deep. —Psalm 64:6

Seek God and God's strength; seek God's presence continually. —Psalm 105:4

Centering Prayer

In breath: "God of all creation . . ."

Out breath: ". . . awaken me to your presence."

Sacred Reflections

What memories do you have of being fully present—to a person, a place, or an object?

When have you experienced being truly yourself? What contributes to those moments?

During what daily activity could you begin (or continue) to practice mindfulness?

Mandala Meditation

Prop up the picture of Anne's dahlia quilt near your candle. Light the candle and sit comfortably before it. For a few moments, be mindful of only your breathing, of each in breath and each out breath. Continue to give about one-quarter of your attention to your breathing and about three-quarters of your attention to noticing the dahlia quilt. Look deeply at its outer edge, the diamond shapes large and small. Notice each concentric circle of diamonds as you let your eyes travel from the outer edges inward towards the center. What colors stand out for you? What sense of the quilt do you discover? What feelings does the mandala evoke for you today? Bring to mind the ways in which this quilted dahlia is connected to others and to the world.

Close your eyes and rest in the image of the mandala. Offer prayers of thankfulness for moments of presence, the creator of the quilt, her mother, all people, and all kinds of flowers.

• Transformation •

ransformation can be gradual or sudden. One of the transforming moments in my life was a mixture of both. The setting was a church camp. Our staff was there for several days of retreat time, although one look at the agenda told me there would be little Sabbath and lots of work. Oh well, we were out of town, in an informal setting, and, as the newest member of the team, I was looking forward to getting to know my colleagues better. Tom Dipko, the conference minster and head of our staff, led opening worship. For the first time in my life, at the age of thirty-seven, I experienced a time of worship in which I felt completely included, welcomed, and loved. The language and the music and the images of that service, while not overtly feminine, took into account my experience of God and my own deep knowing. With that service, my life was transformed. I felt "at home" in worship, for the first time ever.

Without consciously realizing how deeply abandoned I had been feeling, I had brought to that retreat my excessively weary, feminist soul. For years I had been a proponent of inclusiveness for all people, especially in worship and church education. My absolute dedication to using inclusive language for God and God's people had been birthed at least a decade before. I had fought for women to be "allowed" to serve as ushers, deacons, and elders in the church. Having grown up in the Presbyterian tradition, I had agonized with my gay brothers and lesbian sisters when, after years of study and a majority report to the contrary, the national meeting of the Presbyterian General Assembly adopted the minority report of the study group, rejecting ordination for gay and lesbian people.

As of that night of the retreat, I had been a member of the United Church of Christ for five years, propelled into their midst by their inclusive language Book of Worship, their commitment to social justice, and their long history of ordaining and welcoming gay and lesbian people. However, I had never before experienced a service of worship that was totally, gently, wonderfully inclusive. I should have known, perhaps, what to expect. Tom Dipko had served as the editor and chief contributing author to the Book of Worship. Nevertheless, I was completely "blown away" that evening. My dispirited soul suddenly felt hope, gratefulness coursed through my entire body, and a new vision of what might yet be was born. The internal transformation was probably evidenced only by my silent tears, but the memory of that evening has revived me many times since in the ongoing struggle for inclusivity—in the church and beyond.

SACRED STORY

Bailey Cunningham, in writing about mandalas and transformation, shares these reflections:

Mandala-making can serve as an activity for meditation and relaxation or, if we dare to explore deeper aspects of our psyche, it becomes a tool for transformation. . . . Using the mandala as a tool for transformation requires a willingness to surrender both to the process and to ourselves. Relinquishing cherished beliefs in exchange for new meanings and values is often a challenging task. . . . Whatever meets us on our journey to the center gives us a new perspective, a fresh view of an old situation, or a symbol to remind us that we are always engaged in a process of transformation.[1]

In speaking of the transformation required to "be yourself," Henri Nouwen encouraged readers to think of the great teacher, Jesus, who "offered a new model: the circle, where God lives in full solidarity with the people and the people with one another. . . ."[2]

However transformation comes into our lives, for a quilter that transformation will very likely show up in her or his art. Christine Klinger, in telling the story of making her quilt "Tertulia," describes a transforming experience in Santa Fe:

"For most of a decade, I made quilts by following traditional patterns—Bow Tie, Churn Dash, Bear's Paw—designs with a connection to the pioneer past. Gradually, the rhythmic ritual of cutting, arranging and sewing brought forth a desire to give voice to my interior world, to give birth to original designs. Not to copy, but to create. Then a visit to Santa Fe, New Mexico, opened wide the door to a spiritual universe. My quilt making and I were forever transformed.

"The city of Santa Fe has a crazy-quilt culture all its own, where the Hispanic, Anglo and Native American influences blend in a unique and energetic way. Upon visiting this awe-inspiring and wondrous place, I felt compelled to create a quilt that expressed all I had experienced and seen—embroidered roses, plazas, chenille, the Virgin of Guadalupe, milagros, retablos, Navajo weavings, santos, bultos, Diana Bryar note cards, reliquaries, mariposas, Spirit. . . . For me this was the quilter's equivalent of the Annunciation. It was as if God had whispered in my ear and said, 'Go forth, my child, and create a quilt. Share with all the world all I have revealed to you.'

"Without hesitation, I accepted this call to creativity and, as soon as I returned home, enthusiastically began work on the quilt. The birthing of this quilt would have a gestation and due date of its own! I also sensed that this call to quilt making would require me to take risks, develop new technical skills, and become a more patient, reflective quilter. What could not be foreseen was that this three-year creation process would result in the twin birth of an award-winning quilt and a spiritual metamorphosis.

"After visiting Santa Fe, I did not at first fully appreciate how deeply and profoundly I had been affected by this journey. While all of the colors, visual textures, folk and sacred art images had flooded me with inspiration, only eventually was I able to see also how traveling to Santa Fe had enabled me to reconnect with a lost part of my soul. For me, this trip was a spiritual pilgrimage that began a personal transformation, gradually empowering me to quit a no longer satisfying twenty-year career and embark on a path to rediscover and reside with my true, authentic self. Simultaneously, it fostered an ever-deepening creative and spiritual dimension in my life, which even now continues to provide me with immeasurable gifts.

"Amidst the creation of the quilt's border, the word 'tertulia' floated into consciousness. A Spanish/English dictionary offered me this definition: 'an evening gathering or party.' I knew immediately this word, a divine gift, was the perfect name for a celebratory quilt. The creation of 'Tertulia' is my tribute to Santa Fe, as well as a visual and textile testimony to the infinite possibility of spiritual transformation. In giving birth to this quilt, a new self was born—one in which its spirit, just like the quilt's appliqué rose, blossomed when the center was expanded and allowed to grow further out into its borders."

SACRED QUILT

*"Tertulia" by Christine Klinger. Machine pieced, appliquéd,
embellished, and quilted by hand. Created in celebration of Santa Fe,
New Mexico, and the power of spiritual transformation.*

SACRED MEDITATION

Sacred Text

Do not be conformed to this world, but be transformed by the renewing of your minds, so that you may discern what is the will of God—what is good and acceptable and perfect. —Romans 12:2

Centering Prayer

In breath: "In my turning, Holy Sister . . ."
Out breath: ". . . hold me close."

Sacred Reflections

What has inspired transformation in your life?

What colors or symbols speak to you of transforming moments?

How do you make room for transformation in your life?

Mandala Making

Gather your colorful art supplies or fabric into your sacred space. Light your candle and sit comfortably there. Breathe deeply several times, focusing your gaze on the candle light. When you are ready, close your eyes and invite the Holy One to remind you of a time of transformation in your life. Rest in that memory. Notice any feelings in the part of your body that is your center. Notice, too, any colors or images associated with the memory. If a memory does not come, imagine a yearned-for change you have contemplated.

Ponder, then create an image or symbol of transformation. Work on your mandala as you have time today.

As you create, offer thanks for moments of change and moments of stability in your life.

◦ **Birth** ◦

ew life comes to us in many ways. Sometimes life is literally birthed into our families from our own bodies. The miracle of such moments has no parallel that I have found. Out of the circle of the birth canal spirals a tiny being, blessed and, at first, breathless. Coming to breath, the infant graces us with an immediate awareness of the presence of the Holy One and of the preciousness of life itself. Mandalas of celebration have been created for the joy of such times.

Also, new life may come less literally, yet still from within. Mandalas have long been associated with awakening, with revelations and inspirations that are life changing, that propel the meditator towards birthing a new self or making a new beginning. Carl Jung made mandalas himself and noticed that when his clients used mandalas to express their own feelings, dreams, and experience, their self-discoveries were profound and transformative. However birth and renewal come to us, mandalas can encircle the experience and lead us ever more deeply into and beyond our own sacred center.

SACRED STORY

Capturing many astounding and glorious dimensions of birth and new life, my dear friend Barb Davis tells about her mandala quilt "Joining the Circle of Grandmothers":

"As I witnessed the birth of our first grandchild, John Fletcher Davis (Fletch), in October 2002, I had an overwhelming feeling that this birth was being celebrated by all of the grandmothers in history. I felt that all of Fletch's family members, with us in that labor room and beyond, were accompanied by a cloud of witnesses from generations past and from all around the world. This 'cloud' included the most recently deceased, beloved family members, but also extended far beyond those we knew and loved.

"A deep sense of continuity and global community pervaded that moment for me, with wise women from all cultures declaring their celebration of each new life, no matter the locale. They brought the message that all of life is precious; it is our sacred trust to care for, protect, and guide these new little beings. We must find ways to collaborate, they seemed to declare, and to share, to connect with one another for the future of these wee ones.

"Our second grandson, John Warren Davis, was born five weeks after Fletch's arrival, making both of our own sons new fathers.

"As the impact of Fletch's and John's births was settling in my soul, a seed was germinating in my imagination. Energy was gathering to create a quilt that shared my awe at these two little miracles and my evolving understanding that each life is connected to all life around the globe. The sense that God has indeed created *all* beings in God's image deepened in my spirit. The Way of Peace is the way to 'grow children' well.

"This creative quilting 'pregnancy' lasted about four months! The process of creation happened mostly in 'the dark' as I searched for appropriate images and fabrics that would adequately express my wonder over this new role. There was no specific roadmap—only ideas and great suggestions from family and friends.

"At last a dream provided the images of four women from around the earth who would 'stand in' as representatives for all cultures. They encircle the new grandmother and boys, blessing them and praying for their safety and their nurturance. For my role as grandmother, these wise guides remind me of the need to share the feminine ways of wisdom, of living out of unconditional love and truth. They challenge me to act out of compassion and peace-filled living.

"The quilt grew organically. The mandala proved a 'right' design for the circle of grandmothers and, over a period of weeks, various fabrics and embellishments called out to me to be included. Each time I entered my quilting room, I would experience a sense that these spirits, hanging on my design wall, were calling to me, teaching me of the preciousness and duties of being a grandmother. It was very moving to me to include on the quilt surface symbols of new life and my own maternal heritage, such as the dragonfly and an earring given to me by my mother-in-law before her death. There are labyrinths to represent the wise women in my circle of friends, a Celtic circle for our Anglo heritage, and a purple flower, given to me by a wonderful Peruvian grandmother-friend, Maria.

"A friend recently gave me a plaque in clay that says 'Each time a child is born, so is a grandparent.' The impact of this new role is still growing in me, but the creation of this quilt has been an offering of gratitude for the incredible ways that the Holiest of Holy—with each new life—is born anew in each of us.

"During the week that I was completing this quilt, I had three dreams. The first night, the Native American woman who resides in the quilt came to me in answer to a question about my role as a spiritual companion with others. She simply said, 'You are on the right path. Stay there.' The next night, the [Asian] woman stood before me with a serene smile. She said nothing, but I felt that I was being held in love and deep regard. The third night, an entire circle of women came in the dream. I was so excited about the image that I woke myself up!

"These dreams helped me to realize that these images are more than simple fabric cutouts. We are always surrounded by the unseen energy of the ever-present Spirit of Life in all creation and creativity."

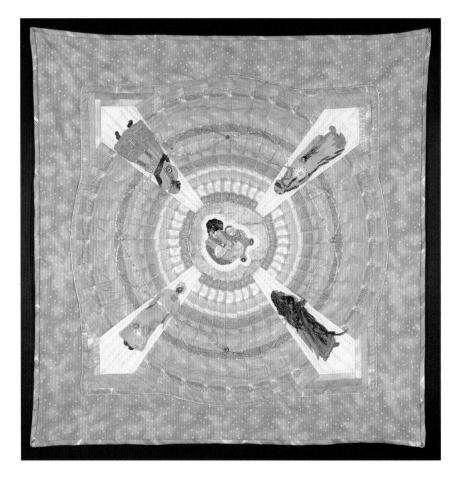

SACRED QUILT

"Joining the Circle of Grandmothers" by Barbara Brewer Davis.
Machine pieced, machine quilted, and hand embellished to celebrate the birth of two grandsons.
Each birth witnessed by grandmother energy from around the world.

SACRED MEDITATION

Sacred Text

For it was you who formed my inward parts; you knit me together in my mother's womb. I praise you, for I am fearfully and wonderfully made. —Psalm 139:13, 14a

Centering Prayer

In breath: "God of All Life . . ."
Out breath: ". . . be born in me anew."

Sacred Reflections

When have you experienced moments of new life or new birth?

    What events or life passages may have precipitated those moments?

    Who has served as a spirit-guide in your life?

Mandala Making

Light your candle and prayerfully sit with Barb's mandala before you. Notice the outer edges of the mandala. Let your eyes travel over each of the grandmothers in the four spokes of the quilt, noticing the details of their dress, culture, and personality. Move your gaze to the center of the quilt, to Barb and her grandsons. Recall your own grandmothers and great-grandmothers, known or unknown, living or deceased. Offer a prayer of thanksgiving for grandmothers and grandfathers of all times and places.

When you have drawn a circle, place in it any images of new life or spirit-guides that come to you as you create. Meditate on the messages they have brought or may be bringing into your life.

Continue to create your mandala as you have time, offering prayers of gratitude whenever you work on it or notice it in your home.

⊙ Passion ⊙

ollow your passion!" With these words, my husband, the career counselor, sums up the essence of his advice to friends struggling with the question "What shall I do with the rest of my life?" Do you love sailing? What part—teaching others to sail? Writing about sailing? Designing the boats? Racing? Find a way to fit that passion into your days or into a significant part of your week. Is your gift teaching? Do you experience a thrill each time you see someone enjoy learning? Each time you know you have helped another person to connect to his or her own inner wisdom in a new way? What age group captivates you? What subject(s)? How can this passion for teaching fit into your life in a major way?

Of course, there are always "buts." "But I trained a long time to be in my present position, invested time and energy into my specialty . . . how could I give all that up now?" "But I have financial commitments, kids in college, a mortgage to pay . . ." "But my spouse has a great job that she loves and we're in a wonderful school district; how could I think about changing all that now?" "But my children still need me to be home with them . . . I want to be home with them . . . and there are only so many hours in a day!"

Change is not easy, even when it applies to our happiness—perhaps *especially* when it applies to our happiness. Following our passion may cost too much: too much comfort, too much disruption, too much strain on our relationships, too much energy, too much separation anxiety. To make a choice for ourselves, to invest in the risk of following a path towards greater happiness and fulfillment, smacks of selfishness. We who are women have been endlessly encouraged to think of others first, to give of ourselves until we are hollowed out, empty. To give voice to our passions, to feelings and "knowings" that run powerfully and intensely within us, is often scary and new. To value ourselves that much, to claim our heritage as created in the image of the Holy One and therefore worthy of our own best efforts may be faithful, but terrifying. Besides, how do we begin such a process?

Not alone: call on your sisters and friends of faith. I have even been known to "check in" with my favorite career counselor! Take time to name aloud your passions and fears. Explore the possibilities. Call on God. Meditate and sit in stillness with your inner knowing. You and God together will envision the way and gauge the journey. As our Quaker friends say, "Way will open." Perhaps your passion will blossom into an innovative career opportunity, or a part-time volunteer ministry. Maybe others in your town share the passion and will join you in a new adventure or offer support as you launch into your own business. There may be guilds or support groups or educational opportunities that match your passion. You might be surprised to find a number of "baby steps" that will start you on a journey towards your larger vision.

As I contemplate the previous paragraph, worrying about whether or not I have just minimized what can be a lengthy, soul-searching process, a phrase comes to me unbidden: "the passion of Christ." In the Christian tradition, we use this phrase during Holy Week, the week immediately preceding Easter, the week during which we retell the stories of Jesus' last ride into Jerusalem, his last supper with the disciples, his arrest, trial, and death, and the miracle of the resurrection. I wonder anew why we use that term, the "passion of Christ," and why Palm Sunday is also called Passion Sunday. I'm sure I've heard it explained numerous times, but today I can recall no specific accounting for the terminology.

Was the Great Teacher, Jesus, following his passion? I can't imagine that he was yearning to sacrifice himself and I have great difficulty with this part of the story, too often used to admonish women about the sacrifices required of us—too often lifted up as a model text for our own selfless giving, giving unto death. No, my soul rejects that yearning as a part of Jesus. Instead, I imagine him feeling passionate about continuing further into the heart of his ministry and mission. He has been ardent about confronting sin and oppression and injustice in the world, about healing the pains and struggles of individuals and society, about announcing anew God's radical love and forgiveness, and about the restoration of humankind's relationship with the Creator. How could he stop now? Yet, how could he go on? Did he know this mission would cost him his life? I have no idea and won't even speculate. Still, riding into Jerusalem, with at least some suspicion of what awaited him there, must have taken remarkable courage, intense determination, and, yes, passion. With the threat of death looming, he remained centered in his mission, confident in God's love for him, and steadfast in his conviction that eventually all would be well.

Believing deeply in what I imagine to have been Jesus' centeredness and confidence, I still have spent several days meditating on whether or not the Holy One led Jesus to his death or would require that of any others of us who might follow our passion. My prayers and reflections lead me here: God calls us into the heart of the world's pain, willing us to use all of our compassion and faith to stand on the side of the oppressed and deprived of the world. God does not call us to death, rather to life and wholeness. God did not will or pre-ordain the death of Jesus, either. Jesus, prayerfully and passionately centered in God's love, chose to lead his followers into "the heart of the world's suffering and struggle."[1] During these days of my own reflections and wrestling with this image of Jesus riding to his death, I "happened" upon these words of Henri Nouwen:

> Give every part of your heart and your time to God and let God tell you what to do, where to go, when and how to respond. God does not want you to destroy yourself. Exhaustion, burnout, and depression are not signs that you are doing God's will. God is gentle and loving. God desires to give you a deep sense of safety in God's love. Once you have allowed yourself to experience that love fully, you will be better able to discern who you are being sent to in God's name.[2]

SACRED STORY

Often expressive of our passions, mandalas may be created to depict "the journey to find one's purpose in life, one's true calling."[3] Quilt artist and mandala creator Dottie Moore describes her journey with mandalas and her quilt "Mandala I" with these words:

"For many years I have drawn mandalas in my journals. They usually appear when I am in transition or feeling overwhelmed by cluttered schedules and commitments. They are circles which I draw and intuitively fill in. They may be in color or black and white. Sometimes they are words that I have written in patterns. I use these drawings to bring me back to center.

"Mandala I" was the first quilt that I made where I worked much like I do when I draw in my journals. It was created in 1997 at a time when I was making many changes in my life and creative work. It represents the fire of passion that I was feeling at the time. The center fire is surrounded by tree images, which represent me and my connection to other women as we bring recognition to the Divine Feminine in the world.

"The colors speak symbolically. Red is the primal color of passion and my connection to the earth. Green is the color of the heart chakra and healing. Yellow is the color of sun energy and the third chakra where we activate our will. Purple represents the spiritual that is found in everything."

SACRED MEDITATION

Sacred Text

Nature teaches a steady lesson: if we want to save our lives, we cannot cling to them, but must spend them with abandon. —Parker Palmer[4]

Centering Prayer

In breath: "Divine Feminine . . ."
Out breath: ". . . illumine my passions within."

Sacred Reflections

What brings you joy?

What are you passionate about?

What do you anticipate as you consider following your passion?

Mandala Meditation

Light a candle and then sit comfortably in your sacred space. Place the photo of Dottie Moore's quilted mandala before you. Close your eyes and breathe deeply for several moments. When you are ready, focus your gaze on the mandala. Starting on the outer edge of the quilt, notice the colors—green, red, and yellow. Let your eyes slowly travel around the design of the yellow circle, pausing at each flame. Notice the

SACRED QUILT

*"Mandala I" by Dottie Moore. Appliquéd, hand painted,
and machine quilted. Created during a major transition for the artist.
Photo by Michael Harrison.*

fine lines of the trees in the red. Notice the purple square and the feminine spirals within the green background. Ponder each tree around the circle. Finally, move your gaze to gently hold the center circle and its sun. Linger in the spiraled center. Notice your own body-center and how you are feeling. Close your eyes and ask for an image of your passion or of God's desire for your life. Open your eyes when you are ready.

Sketch or journal about any of your own images that came. As you end your meditation, offer thanks for the strength of trees, for the fire of passions, for the beauty of this quilt.

∘ Connection ∘

or me, quilts will always be a symbol of connectedness and community. While making a quilt for our daughter's high school graduation, the mystical presence of generations past surrounded me: my great-grandmother who taught me all forms of "hand work," pioneer women who worked by candlelight to create quilts for warmth and beauty, slave women who preserved in cloth the traditions, stories, and symbols of their homeland. At the same time, knowing the quilt I was creating would long outlast my own lifetime, I was conscious of future generations: granddaughters and great-grandchildren on whose bed the quilt might eventually lay, others who would look at the quilt and tell its story in times to come. Connections to the present were vivid for me as well: each stitch contained a blessing, a prayer for my daughter, a hope for her happiness and well-being, a thanksgiving for my grandmother and mother, who continue to make quilts and afghans, and a dream that my daughter would find warm memories and loving Presence whenever she was wrapped in the quilt or slept under it. A "communion of the saints" embodied in one quilt—and not just my daughter's quilt, but every quilt.

In her book *Mandalas: Spiritual Circles for Harmony and Fulfillment*, Laura J. Watts highlights the sense of interconnectedness held sacred by Native Americans:

> Everything contains a spirit, which is the essence of its connection with the world. To walk a path of beauty and truth is to walk in harmony with the spirits among us. . . . One of the most important symbols of the universe is the mandala of the Medicine Wheel. . . . The teaching of the Medicine Wheel is that we will keep moving around the four directions until we can reside in the center. Here we become one with the wheel of life and are in harmony with its ever changing patterns.[1]

In creating her many mandala quilts, Sheila Finklestein, quilt teacher and author of *Magic Quilted Mandalas*, has experienced healing, mystery, and insight. She offers these words of reflection on her mandala quilt, "Prosperity Through Partnership":

"Long before webs and circuits, many ancient peoples recognized the interconnectedness of all things. They knew in their hearts—without quantitative proofs—that Spirit existed and that all creation was connected to *and* through it. They knew that in their own circles of existence, their tribes, each had a contribution to make to the community, that their community was a sum of many parts, a partnership that impacted all within it.

"These ancient people developed symbols to reflect that oneness. Remarkably, those symbols are very similar. For example, separated by thousands of miles and hundreds of years, the Celts of Britain and the First Nations natives of North

America each developed a circular symbol with a central linear axis, connecting the circular arc to its center. These symbols, the Celtic Cross and the Medicine Wheel, continue to exist in our day, in art, architecture, and literature.

"In our culture today, tribes are often dismissed as archaic, and Spirit as superstition, but the benefits of partnerships and interconnectedness continue to hold merit in business and political circles. Creating networks and forming partnerships to work towards common goals benefit both the partners involved and the communities they represent."

Thich Nhat Hanh says it this way: "Poverty and oppression bring war. . . . The fate of each country is linked to the fate of all others. . . .The only way to end the danger is for each of us to do so, and to say to others, 'I am your brother.' 'I am your sister.' 'We are all humankind, and our life is one.'"[2]

SACRED STORY

Sheila continues to tell the story of her quilt with these words:

"The materials for this 'Partnership' mandala had been haunting the pile next to my active projects for several months. They were the remnants of another project and their intricate weblike design and rich, glowing colors continued to intrigue me. They weren't finished with me yet! When approached to do this new mandala quilt, I immediately knew that a medicine wheel was calling from that pile, in a size to be determined by those remnants. Wedge shapes and their duplicates appeared quickly and, surprisingly, in just the correct quantity from very limited yardage. The crosslike spokes, eked from slivers of the leftovers, anchored and focused the medicine wheel. A small central square appeared, the mortal surrounded by the spirit realm. Antique buttons, shining star beads, and other jewelry findings—all spoke to me of the blessings and obstacles on our pathways through life."

SACRED QUILT

"Prosperity Through Partnership" by Sheila Finklestein.
Machine pieced and machine quilted. Created in the Medicine Wheel design and tradition,
with leftover fabric from another mandala quilt.

SACRED MEDITATION

Sacred Text

Where you go, I will go; where you lodge, I will lodge; your people shall be my people, and your God my God. —Ruth 1:16b

Centering Prayer

In breath: "Spirit among us . . ."
Out breath: ". . . connect me to all."

Sacred Reflections

When have you experienced a sense of interconnectedness with nature?

In what ways does your spirit connect to the Divine Spirit? To the spirit of others?

Where do you find community in your life? In your faith?

Mandala Making

Gather drawing or fabric supplies around you and prop Sheila's mandala quilt before you. Light your candle and take several deep, calming breaths. Repeat several times the preceding centering prayer or a prayer of your own heart.

Soften your gaze and take in the whole design of the quilt. Notice the cross. Notice the four quadrants, one at a time. Notice the colors of the mandala and how each makes you feel. Let your gaze linger where it seems drawn.

Close your eyes and invite an image of connection or community. Wait patiently, trusting that one will come. Welcome whatever image you receive and draw or sketch it within a mandala circle. Begin to add fabric to the image, if you choose, or add color with pencils, watercolor, or paint. If an image does not come, try beginning your mandala, open to whatever emerges.

Continue to create your mandala as you have time, offering prayers of thanksgiving for your experiences of community and connection.

• Sacredness •

The sacredness of life is everywhere around me. Throughout the day, I am reminded frequently of the belief shared by our Native American brothers and sisters that every part of creation has a spirit: animals and rocks, trees, people, and bodies of water, the wind, the earth, and all plants. Their habit of offering thanks to the animals, plants, and elements that sacrifice their lives so that others may eat and walk the earth is compelling and testifies to the depth of their belief in the sacredness of all life. The offering of Brachot—prayers of gratitude—is a parallel practice in the Hebrew tradition. Years ago, a Jewish friend taught me to begin these blessing prayers with the traditional words: "Blessed are you, Creator of the Universe, for you have given us . . ." and then to complete the

104

prayer with whatever gratitude I wished to express. When I am mindful of blessings, when gratitude captures my soul, each moment feels sacred and God is nearby.

For all of us, life has a way of getting too busy, too separated from blessings and sacred awareness. Often the problem is not that we lack gratefulness or boundless blessings, rather the problem is distraction and busy-ness that produce an attitude of inattentiveness. Plus, our culture frequently splits the sacred from the everyday, labeling all that is not overtly set apart for holy use as "secular." Mind, body, and spirit are also viewed as separate entities, and polarities are created for "us" and "them," for the "haves" and "have-nots," for "dictatorships" and "democracies," and much more. Fragmentation and polarization can rule the day and permeate our lives.

Perhaps mandalas, as universal symbols of wholeness and unity, are needed more today than ever before. As many of us in the West struggle to regain a sense of centeredness, mandalas invite us into a sacred space of divine energy, a safe place where we might integrate the content of our psyche and the nourishment of our souls. With symbolism that grows out of both universal and personal experience, mandalas offer the possibility of recovering our own true selves and of remembering the Holy One to whom we belong.

Quilting, too, offers possibilities for reclaiming the sacred and for healing. "Sometimes, when all else in life feels out of control or overwhelming, the connection to fabric and design, the familiar rocking motion of stitching, and the spiritual, intimate realization that my foremothers shared the same comfort, re-ground and center my soul. When each stitch is a prayer, or even when each stitch is a release of stress or anger, the sense of the sacredness of life begins again to seep into my consciousness. . . . Quilting often has the mysterious sense of 'coming home,' which I have come to recognize as the return to God, to myself, and to the matters of the world from a position of wholeness or centeredness."[1]

SACRED STORY

The mandalas of our dreams or of our life experience make visible, through their symbolism, our connections to the Holy and our musings about the sacred in our everyday lives. In creating a mandala, especially one in cloth, the creative process is as important as the finished quilt. Susan Schapira describes the process of creating her quilt "Summer Mandala" with these words:

"This quilt had it origins in a meditation on the word 'manifest,' randomly assigned to me in a workshop. As I created the quilt, I focused on the word with this question: How does my spirituality manifest itself in my artwork? That question naturally led to another question: How does my spirituality manifest itself in my daily life? Readings from *365 Tao Daily Meditations* enhanced my understanding that 'our daily lives are our mandala,' meaning that our spirituality is revealed in our everyday actions.

"As a personal challenge, I had purposefully taken a very limited number of fabrics with me to this workshop. I had only six pieces of my hand-dyed fabric and a few fragments of old Indian embroidery. As I meditated more on the meaning of the mandala, the image for this quilt took shape. The raw-edge reverse appliqué designs emphasize the embroidery patterns from India. Rivers run on the diagonal, showing the vitality and creativity that flow through our lives each day.

"This mandala quilt is my focus for meditation in the morning. It is a reminder to me to find daily blessings in the mundane and in the great."

SACRED MEDITATION

Sacred Text

For everything created by God is good and nothing is to be rejected, provided it is received with thanksgiving; for it is sanctified by God's word and by prayer. — I Timothy 4:4–5

Centering Prayer

In breath: "Blessed are you . . ."
Out breath: ". . . Creator of the Universe."

SACRED QUILT

"Summer Mandala" by Susan Schapira. Hand-dyed fabrics, fragments of Indian embroidery, raw-edged reverse appliquéd and machine quilted. Created from reflections on the word "manifest," now used by the artist as a focus for meditation.

Sacred Reflections

How might you reawaken gratitude in your life today?

What helps you notice sacredness?

What would a mandala of sacredness look like for you today?

Mandala Making

Sit or stretch out on the floor near your lighted candle. As you take several deep breaths, relax into the stillness. Close your eyes and call to mind your day so far. Notice blessings and offer thanks for them. Invite images or symbols of things most sacred to you. Rest in those images.

When you are ready, draw a circle and create a mandala of sacredness or blessing. Using your fabric or other art supplies, continue to create this mandala as you have time today. As you go about your day, notice sacred moments or times of blessedness that you might add to your mandala.

As your mandala evolves, offer thanks for all of life and for each sacred part of creation that blesses your day.

• Comfort •

The morning headlines scream of war, a phone call brings word that a beloved church member has died suddenly in her home, and a child cyclist outside on my sidewalk takes a nasty spill, badly skinning both knees. Banking needs to be done, groceries need to be bought, the dogs impatiently await a walk to the park, and my car registration is overdue by eleven days. Words refuse to come as I contemplate writing. The audacity of even trying courses through my being. Usually words give voice to my joy or my pain, to my creativity, to my discomfort, to my very being. Yet, today I wonder who am I to add even one more line, one more paragraph, one more book to the library of the world? Where is comfort or solace this day?

So while the world around me whirls and spins with deep distractions, I contemplate things that bring comfort. Images seep quietly up from my heart:

my older daughter's well-worn teddy bear
a cup of tea
my grandmother's voice
countless sisters and spiritual soul-mates
a quiet sanctuary
my sacred space and quilted candle cloth
my husband's hug
cuddling with our younger daughter
mandalas anchored in my soul
the glory of spring bursting forth
helping hands

The list could continue, of course, with further pondering. But my spirit back-tracks a bit to the word "audacious." I live in a comfortable home, on a tree-lined street, next to many other homes resplendent with front porches and kids we all watch grow up too fast. I do not live in war-torn Iraq, I am not homeless on the streets of our city, I can afford food and clothing and modest vacations. My list of external, physical comforts is endless. What comfort, then, do I seek?

This question is hard; it necessitates more pondering. I try immersing myself in several chores that I might circle back around to the question, give my psyche time to weigh and consider the depths of the comfort I seek. My initial response seems too obvious, too simple. I keep contemplating, overnight and in the morning. As I sit before my candle, it comes to me that I have been distracted by self-doubt and con-sumed by a need to somehow "get it right." So, I sit deep into my own knowing, lis-ten intently to my own inner wisdom, and return to the "simple" response of yesterday. The comfort I seek is God. Or in the true voice of my inner self, "Goddess." I want to live where the Holy One is ever present. I want to return to her arms when I am distressed, lean into her strength when the world seems obsessed with destruction. Both in the quiet of my solitude and in the din of everyday life, I need to know her presence. This is the comfort I seek: this holding, strong, always present Sacred Sister, Loving Spirit, Holy Mother.

The comfort that comes from writing those words is immediate. The Holy One is so much more than my words or images of her, so much more than gender or language can describe, and yet, to be able to name my experience of her is a blessing and a comfort. Others will name their experience of God in various ways, with words and images that bring them comfort. It is the comfort, I believe, that we seek, the knowing of the only one who is the Great Comforter.

What then of discomfort? As I strive to befriend all that is within me, the shadow as well as the light, what is the place of discomfort in my life? How do I deal with the many times when I do not live where God is, do not find her comfort immediate and accessible? Lessons from classes in faith development and psychology come to mind. A person moves to a new level of faith and development when challenged by problems or issues that he or she cannot resolve at the present level. I remember, for example, the years at seminary when whether or not to ordain gay and lesbian people was hotly debated. Basically, I avoided the issue at first. It did not concern me. I was busy commuting, studying, working part-time, holding my life together as I followed this strange new calling to ministry. Then, one evening in my second year of seminary, a dear friend trusted me with the story of her coming out as a lesbian. For a brief moment I was uncomfortable. What was I to say? How was I to respond? What did I really believe? Had I been blind to her pain all of these months of our friendship? And I was embarrassed by my discomfort. But as I dared to look into her eyes again, I was transformed. I saw only grace there. She had not suddenly become someone else. She was still the same incredible child of God she had been before her revelation to me. She was still the friend I had come to cherish and love.

I could no longer be uninvolved or unconcerned about the rights of my lesbian sisters and gay brothers. And in knowing more of their stories, joys, pains, and journeys of faith, my own knowing was transformed. Challenge and discomfort gave way to growth and to experiences of deepened faith. The blessing of discomfort in my life seems to be growth and learning.

SACRED STORY

Mandalas, too, bring us to comfort, with their ability to remind us of wholeness and the way they call us to healing and peace. Sherry Boram describes her mandala quilt "Gloria Mundi" with these words:

"Circles have long held appeal for me because they represent a common form in nature: sun, moon, Earth, sand dollar, sunflower. Circles also symbolize cycles in life: day and night, drought and flood, winter and summer, wakefulness and sleep, hope and despair, health and illness, life and death, beginnings and endings. Mandalas appear in many different cultures and express wholeness and serve as tools for centering.

"The fabric from which I made this quilt sang to me. Though I had no specific design plan in mind when I brought it home, the mandala was a natural choice. It became a quilt that brought me unexpected comfort and pleasure while it was taking form. It still has that effect each time I see it."

SACRED MEDITATION

Sacred Text

I, I am [s]he who comforts you; why then are you afraid of a mere mortal who must die, a human being who fades like grass? —Isaiah 51:12

Centering Prayer

In breath: "Comforting One . . ."
Out breath: ". . . may I be wherever you are."

SACRED QUILT

*"Gloria Mundi" by Sherry Boram. Machine pieced and quilted,
embellished with decorative threads and beads. This quilt, meaning "Glory of the Earth,"
was inspired by circles and patterns in nature and life.*

Sacred Reflections

What is the comfort you seek?

> When have you experienced great comfort? Extreme discomfort?
> What images of God bring you comfort?

Mandala Meditation

Light a candle and then sit comfortably in your sacred space. Place the photo of Sherry's quilted mandala before you. Close your eyes and breathe deeply for several moments.

When you are ready, focus your gaze on the mandala. Starting on the outer edge of the circle, notice the colors and designs you see there. Let your eyes slowly travel around that outer edge. Shift your gaze to the next circle inward. Notice the colors and design. Slowly let your eyes travel around that circle. Moving inward, repeat this meditative gaze until you reach the center of the mandala. Notice the colors and designs in the center. Let your gaze rest there. Remember that to ancient peoples, as well as to our contemporaries, God resides in the mandala's center. As you continue to gaze at the center, invite into your meditation any images of the Divine that bring comfort to you. Close your eyes and allow those images to float across your mind until one seems to sparkle or claim your attention more than the others. Hold that image before you and rest in God. Rest as long as you need, until a sense of comfort claims you. Offer prayers of praise and thanks for all that comforts and restores your soul.

From this place of rest and comfort, call to mind all that brings unrest in your life. Imagine conversing with God about just one of these discomforts. Be very still and listen for God's response in you—perhaps a word, a feeling, a phrase, a comfort. Continue the dialogue until all of your discomforts have been named before the Holy One, until you have listened from a place of deep stillness to God's replies. If you have no experience of holy responses, have no fear. God has listened.

As you open your eyes again, imagine your image of the Holy One residing at the center of Sherry's mandala quilt. Put one hand on your own center, wherever you imagine that to be in your body. Place your other hand on the mandala's center. Close your eyes briefly. Breathe deeply and "anchor" the mandala's center in your own. Rest in that anchoring pose.

When you are ready, end your meditation by offering thanks for the beauty of the world and of Sherry's quilt. During the rest of the day, take occasional opportunities to place your hand over your own center, calling to mind the image of the mandala's center and the Holy One who resides there.

Offer sacred comfort to others and to yourself this day.

• Divinity •

The center of a Tibetan Buddhist mandala is considered to be a dwelling place for the divine. "It can generally be said that Tibetan mandalas are created with the intention of inviting, containing, honoring, and integrating certain kinds of energy exemplified in gods and deities."[1] During meditation, a Buddhist monk mentally travels through the levels of the mandala "palace," encountering guardians and deity along the way to the center, where a Buddha and enlightenment await. In a similar way, a labyrinth offers a pathway to the center, to one's own sacred self. Quilting, too, often described as "soul work," can take us deep into our own selves, into our creativity, imagination, and experiences of God. As with all artists, when we create, we act in the image of the great Creator. Swiss psychologist C. G. Jung introduced mandala artistry to the West as an experiential way to help people connect more deeply to themselves. Jung believed that the psyche, represented by the mandala, held at its center the true self. Experiences of God are central to mandalas, circles, labyrinths, and art.

Naming our own experiences of God, wherever we find them, is important. Who is God to me? What is the nature of the Holy One whom I meet within and beyond? A significant part of our lifelong, spiritual journey centers around our exploration of those two questions. As I quilt, or walk a labyrinth, or reach out to serve another, I experience God in ways that add deep meaning to my life, in ways that may demand a new name to match the experience. Joyous One, Forgiver of All, Goddess of Peace, Creator, Life-Giver, Holy Mother . . . these are but a few of the names that only begin to express my experience of God. As that list of sacred names expands, so does my image of the Divine, so does my understanding of God's nature. An experience of the presence of God cannot be completely contained in any title, but naming the reality of the transcendent in my own life often lifts me to joyfulness and to a deeper "knowing" of the Holy One.

SACRED STORY

Several years ago, my classmates and I were nearing the end of our training program in spiritual direction. We were given the assignment of creating a "synthesis project." After two and a half years of intensive study, reflection, and practice, we were to use our medium of choice to express the summation and integration of our journey and our formation as spiritual directors.

The "medium of choice" part was easy. A quilted project would be fun to create and would prompt reflection on my emerging identity as a spiritual director. Expressing my soul, how I had come to be formed and transformed by the class, was decidedly more challenging. Mandalas had already become an important, sacred symbol in my spiritual journey, so I began drawing circles. The center would be important, expressive of my own heart, intuition, and healing. During the months and years of the class, I had forayed into that center many times, discovered both wisdom and pain within, and had come to deeply treasure the call "home" to my own sacred self. In many ways, the journey toward the ministry of spiritual direction was a reaffirmation of my gifts and a reclaiming of my own voice.

All of that seemed to be summarized by a word that kept repeating in my heart: joy. The colors of "joy" would be my favorite purples, the lines would flow, and the images sparkle. Divine, dancing figures emerged in my drawings, three women, and I knew them immediately. Feminine images of God had long ago become central to my connecting to the Holy. These dancing images were my trinity: God, the Mother; God, the Sister; and God, the Holy Spirit. While I had never actually articulated these God-images in class, their presence at my soul's center was undeniable.

Today, as I ponder this mandala quilt, my soul hears these Holy Women call me into their dance. Whirling with them, I discover authentic joy. Authentic self emerges, daring to skip out into the light. I hear their radiant voices affirming my own voice. With this Goddess image lodged deep in my soul, my own voice gains confidence, emerges toward wholeness, claims "the treasure of true self I already possess." My heart soars. Dancing along the way, I remember again that I am indeed created in the image of God, of this Holy Trinity. What a treasure to discover, this joyous reflection of the Divine.

SACRED MEDITATION

Sacred Text

God is the greatest circle of all, the largest embrace in the universe, which holds visible and invisible, temporal and eternal, as one. —John O'Donohue, in *Anam Cara*[2]

Centering Prayer

In breath: "May Your joy and healing . . ."
Out breath: ". . . break forth in me today."

SACRED QUILT

"Dancing Trinity" by Susan Towner-Larsen.
Pieced, quilted, and embroidered by hand, this quilt celebrates the joy
of feminine images of the Divine.

Sacred Reflections

What images of the Divine One are meaningful for you? What names?

Where do you find your greatest joy?

What activities or people nurture joy in you?

How does joy connect to divinity for you?

Mandala Making

Light your candle, then quietly play some music that speaks joy to your heart. Draw a circle. Place the pencil's point in the center of the circle and close your eyes for a few moments, listening to the music or the silence. With your eyes still closed, let the pencil flow in movements that feel joyful. Continue for as long as you are comfortable, then fill in the drawing with colors that "sparkle" and express joy or divinity for you.

As you continue your drawing, offer to yourself, to loved ones, and to God the following blessing prayer:

Deep peace of the quiet earth to you . . .

Deep peace of the healing waves to you . . .

Deep peace of the shining stars to you . . .

Deep peace of a sister's song to you . . .

Deep peace of the Goddess within to you . . .

Deep, holy peace to you.*

This prayer is my adaptation of an old Gaelic blessing and is stitched in sparkling gold thread around the outside of the "Dancing Trinity" mandala.

Unity

I get a cup of tea, make a plane reservation, call my brother. I reheat the cup of tea, answer the phone, let out the dog. Feeling cold, I pull on a sweatshirt, let the dog in, and decide I'm hungry. I fix a small plate of fruit, feed the cat, and open some windows near my desk. I contemplate the blank screen of my computer. I give up on the computer and contemplate my candle instead. As morning slips away, and with it my prime time for reflection and writing, I realize that I have resisted writing this one reflection for weeks, hence leaving it for the very end.

Although I have read and reflected on the topic extensively, something about unity remains intimidating. Unity and harmony are integral to understanding mandalas, so I must "get this right." The audaciousness of even trying comes to mind!

Writing in my journal, however, I come to realize how deeply seeded this intimidation remains, as if I have to "know" unity and harmony in my own life, or "have it all together"—in a way that I know I do not—in order to write about it. I know better and I know these criteria are not ones I have applied elsewhere. Perhaps unity is what my soul longs for the most and finds the most elusive. Perhaps that makes it hardest to write about.

In his book *Anam Cara,* John O'Donohue says, "The soul is wise and subtle; it recognizes that unity fosters belonging. The soul adores unity. What you separate, the soul joins."[1] Deep within, I recognize that yearning towards unity—it's what my soul brings to every mandala and to every quilt. I want to belong to the great tradition of meditation that spans all time and faith expressions. I want to piece my life together into a quilt of harmony and unity that can never come apart. Somehow, mandalas link those two desires, the first of which is possible, the second of which remains a dream.

For this is the truth of the matter: life does not feel unified or harmonious. In the world and within myself, unity seems fleeting, at best. Nations and faith traditions are at war, political parties create enemies and assign aspects of evilness to each other, humankind carelessly continues to decimate nature and its resources, art is grossly underfunded in most communities and sports are grossly overfunded, and neighbors who have little are looked at suspiciously and judgmentally by neighbors who have more. Inside of me dualities clash, as well. How can it be that the persons I love the most are also the ones at whom I can become the most furious, to whom I can behave the most hatefully? While valuing integrity, how is it I still make choices sometimes that are not healthy or "not me"? Inside and out, life can seem very unbalanced and far from harmonious. No wonder my soul continues to long for unity.

As I contemplate that ever-shifting sense of balance within and without, the image of Navajo sand paintings comes to mind.

The Navajo believe that illness arises through disharmony with the world. . . . A medicine man (or woman) cures the sick by re-balancing their lives. The healer performs a ceremony, or Way, which is a carefully constructed pathway that brings the patient to a place of wholeness and releases illness. The Way is centered on a mandala sand painting, the symbol of balance and harmony, and its story. . . . The medicine man chants or sings the story of the pathway back to harmony . . . the spirits draw down the illness so that it falls into the mandala . . . (the sand) is ritually disposed of so that the healed person is free to walk a new path of health.[2]

A sigh goes through my soul just imagining such a Way and I begin to breathe again, deeply and with hope. My memory shifts to two other faith traditions that use the language of "the way": early Christians were known as people of "the Way" and Quakers speak of "way opening" or "way closing." Unity, I am beginning to think, has something to do with finding my way—my way home, my way in the midst of dualities, my way to God.

The beautiful, symmetrical Tibetan sand paintings—mandalas of incredible detail—also represent pathways that lead to unity and harmony. The Wheel of Time mandala, one of the most intricate, offers a "path to enlightenment . . . all the wisdom of the cycles of the universe and the healing that comes from living in harmony with its unceasing rhythms."[3] Tibetan monks memorize and prayerfully "walk through" the details of this mandala, which represents "the flat version of a five-story palace in which the Kalachakra Buddha lives."[4]

Such pathways into contemplation remind me of labyrinths, another form of mandala created for walking meditation. Lauren Artress, creator of the Labyrinth Project and author of *Walking a Sacred Path*, tells a story in her book about a community that came together to create and tend a labyrinth, one that was as much garden as pathway. Dr. Artress sees such community efforts as a way to break down barriers between people and points to a similar effort at communication, newly begun, between scientists and mystics. "This is a great cause for celebration. This reunion of science and religion can lead us out of the severe divisions of our chaotic times. . . . We need a vision of unity, we need to realize that we are all on the path together. We need to join together in a communal prayer for ourselves and for our planet."[5] Wow! Hers are a vision, a path, and a prayer that capture my soul and begin to heal my sense of unbalance. As I sit in silence with that vision of unity, I breathe deeply. Coming full circle, I am reunited with a hope, with the Sacred One, and with myself.

SACRED STORY

At first sight of Barbara Stover's mandala quilt, my soul shifted into calmness. My gaze rested on the center point of her mandala, equally distant from every other point of the mandala's outer curve. The monochromatic color scheme suggests unity, wholeness, purity. She describes her mandala with these words:

"This is one of my favorite mandalas because it speaks for itself, without the support of fabric designs. In the planning stages, I wondered if such a design could be done. I experimented with trapunto and white fabric. Quilted entirely by machine, it is very heavily embellished with white, clear, pearl, and iridescent beads and ribbon. I am very happy to have the results.

"Mandalas, as an inspiration, have given me a creative outlet, engaged my mind, and focused my energies. My pieces, whether square or round, are heavily embellished and feature circle motifs. They are usually not preplanned, but rather grow from a central point inspired by beautiful fabrics. This uncharted process with no set goal, size, or idea in mind allows me to add elements—as discoveries are made or as fancy strikes. The embellishment process is a peaceful endeavor for me. It allows time for creative sparks and personal reflection. With the embellishment comes diversity, from beads that are barely seen, yet sparkle, to large, chunky pieces that serve as a design focus. Once finished, the adorned pieces demand to be studied, enjoyed, and even touched.

"Each mandala I create has a personal significance, most often reflecting the current happenings in my life. My work is a meditation, concentrating on the careful placement of each element in the design. I strive to create balance and harmony for the elements and for myself."

SACRED MEDITATION

Sacred Text

When you come patiently and silently home to yourself, you come into unity and into belonging.
—John O'Donohue, in *Anam Cara*[6]

Centering Prayer

In breath: "Holy One . . ."
Out breath: ". . . bless my vision of unity."

Sacred Reflections

What dualities or opposites do you find in your world? Do you hold within your self?
In what ways might you value both the light and the shadow within your self?
What images speak to you of unity and harmony? What practices?

Mandala Meditation

Prop the picture of Barbara Stover's mandala quilt near your candle. Light the candle and sit comfortably before it. For a few moments, close your eyes and be mindful of only your breathing, of each breath in and each breath out.

When you are still, open your eyes and gaze at the mandala quilt, continuing to give about one-quarter of your attention to your breathing and about three-quarters of your attention to noticing the quilt. Focus your eyes on the mandala's center. Notice, then release any thoughts that may come to you and remain focused on the mandala. Expand your gaze to include the entire quilt. After a few moments, focus on the outer edge. Slowly move your gaze inward, giving your eyes time to find a path to the center. Pause whenever you need to. Once in the center, close your eyes again. Call to mind the mandala. Imagine it as a source of white, radiant Light, shining directly into your heart. Rest in that Light.

As you end the meditation, give thanks for the opposites within you and give thanks for moments of unity, balance, and harmony in your life.

SACRED QUILT

"Like a Virgin . . . Mandala 11" by Barbara Stover. Designed, machine quilted, and embellished by the artist. Inspired by the history of beautiful white-on-white quilts and the desire to produce the next step in that tradition.

ENDNOTES

INTRODUCTION

1. Joyce Rupp, *The Star in My Heart* (Philadelphia: Innisfree Press, 1990), 21.

MEDITATION

1. Joan Borysenko, *Pocketful of Miracles* (New York: Warner Books, 1994), 7.
2. Ibid., 22.
3. Ibid., 75. (Note: Patanjali was the first recorder of oral poems of instruction in yoga meditation.)

CIRCLES

1. John O'Donohue, *Anam Cara* (New York: HarperCollins, 1998), 162–63.
2. Sue Bender, *Stretching Lessons* (New York:, HarperCollins, 2001), 94.
3. Bailey Cunningham, *Mandala, Journey to the Center* (New York: DK Publishing, 2002), 42.
4. Quoted in John O'Donohue, *Anam Cara* (New York: HarperCollins, 1998), 192.

CENTERING

1. Susan Towner-Larsen and Barbara Brewer Davis, *With Sacred Threads* (Cleveland: United Church Press, 2000), 77–78.
2. Quoted by Catherine Whitmire, *Plain Living* (Notre Dame, Ind.: Sorin Books, 2001), 21.

JOURNEY

1. Lauren Artress, *Walking a Sacred Path* (New York: Riverhead Books, 1995), xii.
2. Thich Nhat Hanh, *Peace Is Every Step* (New York: Bantam Books, 1991), 28.

DREAMS

1. Laura J. Watts, *Mandalas* (London: Hermes House, 2000), 15.

BALANCE

1. Joan Borysenko, *Pocketful of Miracles* (New York: Warner Books, 1994), 69.

BLESSING

1. Joan Borysenko, *Pocketful of Miracles* (New York: Warner Books, 1994), 419.
2. Bailey Cunningham, *Mandala, Journey to the Center* (New York: DK Publishing, 2002), 15.
3. Ibid.

LIGHT

1. Lizzie Cowperthwaite, "Mandala." Used with permission.

SHELTER

1. Thames and Hudson, Ltd., *Sacred Symbols: Mandala* (New York: Thames and Hudson, 1995), 12.
2. Ibid., 19.
3. Susanne F. Fincher, *Creating Mandalas* (Boston: Shambhala Publications, 1991), 139.

CREATION

1. Thich Nhat Hanh, *Peace Is Every Step* (New York: Bantam Books, 1991), 106.
2. Thames and Hudson, Ltd., *Sacred Symbols: Mandala* (New York: Thames and Hudson, 1995), 10.

PEACE

1. William Sloan Coffin, *A Passion for the Possible* (Louisville, Ky: Westminster John Knox Press, 1993), 10.
2. Joan Borysenko, *Inner Peace for Busy People* (Carlsbad, Calif.: Hay House, 2001), 5.
3. Ibid., 7.
4. Bailey Cunningham, *Mandala, Journey to the Center* (New York: DK Publishing, 2002), 6.
5. *The New Century Hymnal* (Cleveland: Pilgrim Press, 1995), 563.

HEALING

1. Parker J. Palmer, *Let Your Life Speak* (San Francisco: Jossey-Bass, 2000), 69.
2. From Tarthang Tulku, in *Mandala Gardens,* quoted by Sheila Finklestein, *Magic Quilted Mandalas* (Iola, Wisc.: Krause Publications, 1999), 7.

PRESENCE

1. Thich Nhat Hanh, *Peace Is Every Step* (New York: Bantam Books, 1991), 43–44.
2. Ibid., 44.

TRANSFORMATION

1. Bailey Cunningham, *Mandala, Journey to the Center* (New York: DK Publishing, 2002), 76.
2. Henri J. M. Nouwen, *The Inner Voice of Love* (New York: Doubleday, 1998), 41.

PASSION

1. Susan Blain, ed., *Imaging the Word* (Cleveland: United Church Press, 1996), 153.
2. Henri J. M. Nouwen, *The Inner Voice of Love* (New York: Doubleday, 1998), 106.
3. Bailey Cunningham, *Mandala, Journey to the Center* (New York: DK Publishing, 2002), 119.
4. Parker J. Palmer, *Let Your Life Speak* (San Francisco: Jossey-Bass, 2000), 105.

CONNECTION

1. Laura J. Watts, *Mandalas: Spiritual Circles for Harmony and Fulfillment* (London: Hermes House, 2000), 14, 15.
2. Thich Nhat Hanh, *Peace Is Every Step* (New York: Bantam Books, 1991), 119.

SACREDNESS

1. Susan Towner-Larsen and Barbara Brewer Davis, *With Sacred Threads* (Cleveland: United Church Press, 2000), 78.

DIVINITY

1. Susanne F. Fincher, *Coloring Mandalas* (Boston: Shambhala Publications, 2000), 6.
2. John O'Donohue, *Anam Cara* (New York: HarperCollins, 1998), 228.

UNITY

1. John O'Donohue, *Anam Cara* (New York: HarperCollins, 1998), 118.
2. Laura J. Watts, *Mandalas* (London: Hermes House, 2000), 16–17.
3. Ibid, 20.
4. Ibid, 21.
5. Lauren Artress, *Walking a Sacred Path* (New York: Riverhead Books, 1995), 126.
6. O'Donohue, *Anam Cara,* 120.

ANNOTATED BIBLIOGRAPHY OF RELATED RESOURCES

BOOKS ABOUT QUILTED MANDALAS

Dales, Judy. *Curves in Motion*. Lafayette, Calif.: C&T Publishing, 1998.
"The Gallery" contains several beautiful mandala quilts, created using Judy Dale's curved seam techniques, taught in the book. Judy's own circular quilts, throughout the book, are gorgeous.

Finklestein, Sheila. *Magic Quilted Mandalas*. Iola, Wisc.: Krause Publications, 1999.
In the introduction, Sheila writes about the mysticism of the mandala and its healing impact in her own life. Most of this book, however, is about how to make mandala quilts using a wedge ruler and striped fabric.

Pasquini, Katie. *Mandala Quilt Designs*. New York: Dover Publications, 1983.
Again, in its introduction, this book mentions some of the origins and uses of mandalas, yet is focused mainly on how to construct quilted mandalas.

Pignatelli, Vikki. *Quilting Curves*. Lincolnwood, Ill.: Quilt Digest Press, 2001.
  Although not about mandalas specifically, the curved piecing technique Vikki
  teaches is a help in creating any quilted art with curves and circles.

Sudo, Kumiko. *Circles of the East*. Lincolnwood, Ill.: Quilt Digest Press, 1997.
  Quilt designs for kamons, ancient and circular Japanese family crests. Especially
  for those who like to appliqué.

Williams, Beth Ann. *Celtic Quilts: A New Look for Ancient Designs*. Woodinville, Wash.:
  Martingale & Company, 2000.
  Beth Ann's techniques and many of her designs offer yet more inspiration for mandalas.

BOOKS ABOUT MANDALAS

Blau, Tatjana. *Tibetan Mandalas*. New York: Sterling Publishing, 1998.
  A book of Tibetan mandala designs.

Cornell, Judith. *Mandala: Luminous Symbols for Healing*. Wheaton, Ill.: Quest Books, 1994.
  An extensive look at mandalas, how to create them for healing and renewal, their
  spiritual significance. Truly luminous mandalas.

Cunningham, Bailey. *Mandala: Journey to the Center*. New York: DK Publishing, 2002.
  Beautiful, informative. If you can only buy one mandala book, make it this one.

Fincher, Susanne. *Creating Mandalas*. Boston: Shambhala Publications, 1991.
  About mandalas and their symbolism.

_____. *Coloring Mandalas*. Boston: Shambhala Publications, 2000.
  Excellent, concise background on mandalas and actual designs to color and enjoy.

Holitzka, Klaus. *Mandalas of the Celts*. New York: Sterling Publishing, 1996.
  Celtic mandala designs to color.

_____. *Native American Mandalas*. New York: Sterling Publishing, 1998.
  A book of Native American mandala designs.

Jung, Carl. *Mandala Symbolism*. Princeton, N.J.: Princeton University Press, 1972.
Jung's understandings of the therapeutic and psychic uses of mandalas, details and examples of mandalas, their symbolism and interpretations.

Leidy, Denise Patry, and Robert A. F. Thurman. *Mandala: The Architecture of Enlightenment*. New York: Asia Society Galleries, 1997.
From a pan-Asian exhibition of mandalas, intended to highlight the symbolism as well as the artistry of these Hindu-Buddhist "sacred cosmograms."

Mandali, Monique. *Everyone's Mandala Coloring Book*. Volumes 1, 2, 3. Billings, Mont.: Mandali Publishing, 1991.
Beautiful designs for adults and children to color. Great for those who may be hesitant at first to create their own mandalas. Lots of other mandala resources at her website: www.mandali.com.

Merrill, Nan C. *Meditations and Mandalas*. New York: Continuum Publishing, 2002.
Black and white mandala drawings accompany each psalm-like reflection.

Negi, Geshe Lobsang Tenzin, and Lloyd Nick, eds. *The Mystical Arts of Tibet*. Atlanta, Ga.: Longstreet Press, 1996.
Beautiful. The story of Tibet told through its art, including mandalas.

Pilastre, Christian. *Rosaces*. l'Hermitage, St. Sever-Calvados, France: Marie Pre, Publisher, 1979.
A rose-window coloring book, published as a part of a series by a small group of Carmelite nuns in France.

Rupp, Joyce. *The Star in My Heart*. Philadelphia, Pa.: Innisfree Press, 1990.
Reflections, poetry, and prayers on inner wisdom, illustrated by the mandalas of Judith Veeder.

ten Grotenhuis, Elizabeth. *Japanese Mandalas*. Honolulu, Haw.: University of Hawaii Press, 1999.
An extensive study of the sacred symbolism and traditions of Japanese mandalas and their origins.

Thames and Hudson, Ltd. *Sacred Symbols: Mandala.* New York: Thames and Hudson, 1995.
An amazing little book in their "Sacred Symbols" series.

Tharchin, Sermey Geshe Lobsang. *A Commentary on Guru Yoga and Offering of the Mandala.* Ithaca, N.Y.: Snow Lion Publications, 1987.
A guide for yoga meditation, with the three forms of mandala offering: outer mandala, inner mandala, and secret mandala.

Watts, Laura J. *Mandalas.* London: Arness Publishing, 2000.
A treasure of a book, includes symbolism across many cultures and how to create mandalas.

BOOKS ABOUT LABYRINTHS

Artress, Lauren. *Walking A Sacred Path.* New York: Riverhead Books, 1995.
Historical origins and modern day uses of the labyrinth. Wonderful, insightful reflections by the author.

Geoffrion, Jill Kimberly Hartwell. *Praying the Labyrinth.* Cleveland: United Church Press, 1998.
Meditations for labyrinth walking.

_____. *Living the Labyrinth.* Cleveland: United Church Press, 2000.
More and expanded ways to meditate in a labyrinth.

Sands, Helen Raphael. *Labyrinth: Pathway to Meditation and Healing.* London: Gaia Books, 2000.
Symbolism, dance, history, and reflections on labyrinths. Instructions on how to make one.

Schaper, Donna, and Carole Ann Camp. *Labyrinths From the Outside In.* Woodstock, Vt.: Skylight Paths Publishing, 2000.
Reflections, information, and walking meditations for use in labyrinths. Brief directory by state and country on labyrinth locations.

INDEX OF QUILT ARTISTS

Colleen Curry   **Page 54**   **"Tree"**

Machine appliquéd and quilted. Some leaves are silk, with machine embroidery, background leaves are painted. Suspended in an old bass drum hoop and painted blue to represent the sky.

Barbara Brewer Davis   **Page 90**   **"Joining the Circle of Grandmothers"**

Machine pieced, machine quilted, and embellished to celebrate the birth of two grandsons. Each birth is witnessed by grandmother energy worldwide.

Gail Ferrick   **Page 72**   **"Solstice"**

Created to honor the artist's beloved and to mark the beginning of the rest of her life.

Sheila Finklestein   **Page 102**   **"Prosperity Through Partnership"**

Created in the Medicine Wheel design and tradition with "leftover" fabric from another mandala quilt.

Anne Gailhbaud   **Page 78**   **"Dahlia"**

Created to honor the artist's mother, the "queen of the dahlias."

Terry Grant   **Page 60**   **"Earth, Sun, and Moon"**

Fused appliqué, machine quilted, 2002.

Christine Klinger   **Page 84**   **"Tertulia"**

Machine pieced, appliquéd, embellished, and quilted by hand. Created in celebration of Santa Fe, New Mexico, and the power of spiritual transformation.

Dottie Moore   **Page 16**   **"Centering"**

Photo by Michael Harrison—Hand painted, machine and hand embroidered, machine quilted. Commissioned as a healing quilt for a woman challenged with major health issues.

                 Page 97   **"Mandala I"**

Photo by Michael Harrison—Appliquéd, hand painted, and machine quilted. Created during a major transition for the artist.

                 Page 41   **"Where Love Abides"**

Photo by Michael Harrison—From the collection of Andrew Lohmann and Laurie Schoelkopf. Appliquéd, hand painted, hand embroidered. Celebrates the birth of a first child.

Susan Nash   **Page 65**   **"Om—The Sound of Peace"**

Machine pieced, hand appliquéd, and hand beaded. Dye-discharge used to create center symbol.

Susan Schapira   **Page 107**   **"Summer Mandala"** © 1997

Hand-dyed fabrics and fragments of Indian embroidery, raw-edged reverse appliquéd and machine quilted.

Sheila Steers   **Page 22**   **"Walk With Me"**

Hand appliquéd and machine quilted. A challenge quilt interpreting the artist's guild's theme of "Peaceful Reflections." It won first place in that guild's 2002 quilt show.

Barbara Stover   Page 127   **"Like a Virgin ... Mandala 11"**

Designed, machine quilted, and embellished by the artist. Inspired by a history of beautiful white-on-white quilts and the desire to produce the "next step" in that tradition.

Susan Towner-Larsen   Page 119   **"Dancing Trinity"**

Pieced, quilted, and embroidered by hand. It celebrates the joy of feminine images of the Holy.

Larkin Van Horn   Page 49   **"Light One Candle"**

Photo by Mark Frey—Fabric collage and machine embroidered. A meditation on moving out of the darkness and into the light and resting in God.

J. Bruce Wilcox   Page 11   **"New Dawn"**

Machine pieced and hand quilted. Created to mark the completion of one life cycle and the beginning of a new, more powerful, and positive spiritual one.

Beth Ann Williams   Page 28   **"Mandala Series: Dreamtime"**

"Invisible" machine appliqué and machine quilting with variegated rayon thread.

Related titles available from The Pilgrim Press

WITH SACRED THREADS
Quilting and the Spiritual Life
Susan Towner-Larsen and Barbara Brewer Davis

This book is an opportunity to reflect on the endless ways that quilting is a context for the spiritual journey. Each chapter centers on a theme that connects to life in the Spirit and to life as a quilter. Includes beautiful, full-color images of quilts.

ISBN 0-8298-1384-5/Paper/128 pages/$23.00

GODZONE
A Guide to the Travels of the Soul
Mike Riddell

This is a guide to Godzone—the space inhabited by God. It is a book for travelers, who follow an inner urge, a voice that calls from the depths, and a desire to explore the territory. Riddell is the recipient of ForeWord magazine's 2001 Book of the Year Award for *Sacred Journey: Spiritual Wisdom for Times of Transition*.

ISBN 0-8298-1516-3/Paper/112 pages/$11.00

HENRI'S MANTLE
100 Meditations on Nouwen's Legacy
Chris Glaser

Glaser, a student and friend of Nouwen for more than twenty-five years, interprets Nouwen's sacred writings and presents 100 meditations on his words, in the hope that Nouwen's ministry will continue to thrive.

ISBN 0-8298-1497-3/Paper/212 pages/$18.00

IN WISDOM'S PATH
Discovering the Sacred in Every Season
Jan L. Richardson

Richardson takes readers on a remarkable journey through the seasons of the church year to discover Wisdom in all her guises. The search takes various forms—striking full-color images, thoughtful and moving prayers, insightful personal reflections—drawn together as a means to help those struggling to open themselves to God.

ISBN 0-8298-1324-1/Paper/144 pages/$23.00

LABYRINTH AND THE SONG OF SONGS
Jill Kimberly Hartwell Geoffrion

Geoffrion has created a unique spiritual experience—the fourth book in her labyrinth series—cleverly intertwining traditional labyrinthine concepts and the entire Hebrew Scriptures love poem "Song of Songs." This is for the seasoned labyrinth aficionado who wants to take the next step, spiritually speaking. Features illustrations of the labyrinth of Chartres Cathedral in France as well as an original hymn.

ISBN 0-8298-1539-2/Paper/96 pages/$12.00

THE LABYRINTH AND THE ENNEAGRAM
Circling into Prayer
Jill Kimberly Hartwell Geoffrion and Elizabeth Catherine Nagel

Gives readers an orientation in the enneagram and an explanation of the nine positions of attention that affect the ways in which we respond to the sacred and to others. Includes exercises on the labyrinth with scripture references.

ISBN 0-8298-1450-7/Paper/118 pages/$15.00

LIVING THE LABYRINTH
101 Paths to a Deeper Connection with the Sacred
Jill Kimberly Hartwell Geoffrion

This book offers beginners and seasoned labyrinth users a multitude of new ways to approach this sacred tool. The short, devotional-like chapters may be used however the reader chooses—because any way that the labyrinth is approached is the right way.

ISBN 0-8298-1372-1/Paper/88 pages/$17.00

OUTSIDE THE LINES
Meditations on an Expansive God
Andrea La Sonde Anastos

Divided into four sections, *Outside the Lines* is a compelling collection of 19 meditations designed to enhance one's spirituality. It invites readers to claim their own creation in the divine image and can be used as a personal or group spiritual guide.

ISBN 0-8298-1471-X/Paper/160 pages/$13.00

PRAYING THE LABYRINTH

A Journal for Spiritual Exploration

Jill Kimberly Hartwell Geoffrion

This book is a journal that leads readers into the spiritual exercise of self-discovery through scripture selections, journaling questions, and poetry, with generous space for personal reflections.

ISBN 0-8298-1343-8/Paper/112 pages/$15.00

SACRED JOURNEY

Spiritual Wisdom for Times of Transition

Mike Riddell

This book, the author's North American debut, is the recipient of ForeWord magazine's 2001 Book of the Year Award. It is for anyone who has ever asked, "What now?" or "What will be left of my life when I'm gone?" The author brilliantly identifies the malaise that is particularly common in midlife and shows us how to make it a time for focusing on what really matters.

ISBN 0-8298-1456-6/Paper/216 pages/$16.00

To order these or any other books from The Pilgrim Press, call or write to:

The Pilgrim Press
700 Prospect Avenue
Cleveland, OH 44115-1100

PHONE ORDERS: 800·537·3394 (M–F, 8:30AM–4:30PM ET)
FAX ORDERS: 216·736·2206

Please include shipping charges of $4.00 for the first book and 75¢ for each additional book.

Or order from our Web site at www.thepilgrimpress.com.

Prices subject to change without notice.